THE ROAD TO HEAVEN

A Traveler's Guide to Life's Narrow Way

Don Johnson

For Kendra.

I am so glad we get to walk the narrow road together.

CONTENTS

Acknowledgments ix

Introduction Our Situation xiii

Part I: Out of Egypt:
Set Free by God 23

Chapter 1 The Deliverer 25
Chapter 2 Who Is This Man? 33
Chapter 3 Under the Blood of the Lamb 45

Part II: Across the Wilderness:
The Nature of the Journey 61

Chapter 4 The Call to Discipleship 63
Chapter 5 God's Reason for Everything 81
Chapter 6 Faith 105
Chapter 7 Work 133
Chapter 8 Rules and Righteousness 149
Chapter 9 The Seriousness of Sin 169
Chapter 10 The Necessity of Perseverance 193
Chapter 11 God With Us 217

Part III: Into the Promised Land: Practical
                 Tips for a Successful Trip..............235

Chapter 12   The Comfort Trap 237
Chapter 13   The Trustworthiness of God....................255

ACKNOWLEGMENTS

Thanks to the hundreds of people God has put in my path over the years to help me along. Although I cannot name you all on this page, know that you have had a hand in this work. I could not have done it without you.

Thank you also to the young adults of the Evangelical Free Church of Huntington Beach college/career group. Your sharp minds and willingness to talk clarified the ideas in this book.

To Heather Garcia, Amy Leonhardt, Greg Laws, and Brandon Ridley: thank you for your help with the manuscript. Your advice was invaluable.

Finally, a big thank you to my parents for your unwavering support, and for showing me what life on the narrow way is supposed to look like.

Enter through the narrow gate. For wide is the gate and broad is the road that leads to destruction, and many enter through it. But small is the gate and narrow the road that leads to life, and only a few find it.

Matthew 7:13-14

INTRODUCTION

Our Situation

"Is This All There Is?"

Y ou are unsatisfied with your life. Maybe you haven't spent much time thinking about it, but deep down you know it's true. In those rare moments of silence, when you find yourself away from the TV, unplugged from your iPod and on a quick break from work, family, and a long list of social duties, you notice it: a gnawing sense of emptiness and disappointment. In your heart you are trying to come to grips with the fact that life isn't all it is cracked up to be. You want something more.

You are not alone. I am right there with you, as are many, many others. We live in the most affluent, technologically advanced culture the world has ever known, but as a people we are not truly content. Something is missing. As Ilya Shapiro explained in a tcsdaily.com article, he and many of his fellow Gen-xers have achieved a great deal of what the world considers success, but, in the words of U2, they still haven't found what they are looking for.

> [We have made it to the top of our professions] and although it makes us sound like spoiled brats (and me narcissistic for writing about it) – we're not happy. Or, rather, after a (relatively short) lifetime of playing by the rules, eating our greens, graduating from high school, then college, then grad school or whatever other apprenticeship takes up our early-to-mid-20s, and finally starting work in the real world we've come to realize that there's more to life than taking an anointed spot in the meritocracy.
>
> We were told by our parents (and Billy Joel) that if we worked hard, if we behaved, we would achieve the good life. Well, we've achieved! Achieved!! ACHIEVED!!! and now… what?
>
> David Brooks take note: Generation X has arrived, made its presence felt, looked around, and is wondering, "Is that all there is?"
>
> It is a conversation I keep having, or talking around, with my friends and peers – the type of folks who 20 years ago would have been called yuppies (which label I at least am happy to wear now, if in a descriptive rather than ascriptive way). They – we – have everything we could ever want in this stage of life, but still we search for meaning.[1]

Young adults are not the only ones looking for something more. Baby boomers are trying to fill a void in their lives as well. Gregg Easterbrook notes that while his generation's current standard of living far surpasses any of his ancestors', the overall level of happiness has not increased at all: "Suppose your great-great grandparents, who lived four generations ago, materialized in the United States of the present day. Surely they would first be struck by the scale and clamor of present-day life, and might not like these things; neither do we, necessarily." But, "as [they] learned more of contemporary life, they would be dazzled. Unlimited food at affordable prices, never the slightest worry about shortages, unlimited variety – strawberries in March! – so much to eat that in the Western nations, overindulgence now plagues not just the well-off but the poor, the poor being more prone to obesity than the population as a whole."[2]

Easterbrook goes on to point out other aspects of contemporary life that would "strike our recent ancestors as nearly miraculous," such as the 77 year average life span (up from 41 at the beginning of the twentieth century), the defeat of "history's plagues – polio, smallpox, measles, rickets," the end of backbreaking physical toil for most wage earners, instantaneous global communication, same-day travel to distant cities, the end of formal discrimination, mass home-ownership, and incredible advances of freedom. "All told, except for the clamor and speed of society, and for the trends in popular music, your great-great-grandparents might say the contemporary United States is the realization of Utopia."[3]

But it isn't Utopia. Easterbrook concludes by saying that although everything is better, we are not happy.

> Yet how many of us feel positive about our moment, or even believe that life is getting better? Today Americans tell pollsters that the country is going downhill; that their parents had it better; that they feel unbearably stressed out; that their children face a declining future. …

The percentage of Americans who describe themselves as "happy" has not budged since the 1950s,
though the typical person's real income has more
than doubled through that period. Happiness has not
increased in Japan or Western Europe in the past half-
century, either, though daily life in both those places
has grown fantastically better, incorporating all the
advances noted above plus the end of dictatorships
and recovery from war... [Even in an era of abun-
dance and social progress] the citizens of the United
States and the European Union, almost all of whom
live better than almost all of the men and women in
history, entertain considerable discontent.[4]

We have everything we can think of to want, yet we are
not satisfied. In this respect we are just like Solomon, one
of the greatest kings of ancient Israel and writer of the Old
Testament book of Ecclesiastes. He achieved everything he
could think of to achieve and got for himself everything he
could think of to acquire, yet he was still left empty.

I denied myself nothing my eyes desired; I refused
my heart no pleasure. My heart took delight in all my
work, and this was the reward for all my labor. Yet
when I surveyed all that my hands had done and what
I had toiled to achieve, everything was meaningless,
a chasing after the wind; nothing was gained under
the sun. (Ecclesiastes 2:10-11)

He concludes, "So I hated life, because the work that is
done under the sun was grievous to me. All of it is meaningless, a chasing after the wind" (Ecclesiastes 2:17).

The Answer

I will expand on this proposition shortly, but for now let me summarize the biblical answer to our problem. The reason that nothing on earth satisfies our innermost longings is that we do not actually long for anything on earth. As C.S. Lewis argues,[5] "If I find in myself a desire which no experience in this world can satisfy, the most probable explanation is that I was made for another world."[6]

That other world is Heaven.[7] Heaven is what we are missing, what we are longing for. Our deepest problem on earth is that we do not belong here. We were created to live in the presence of God, and existing anywhere else will leave us unfulfilled. In the words of Randy Alcorn, we are homesick.

> Nothing is more often misdiagnosed than our homesickness for Heaven. We think that what we want is sex, drugs, alcohol, a new job, a raise, a doctorate, a spouse, a large-screen television, a new car, a cabin in the woods, a condo in Hawaii. What we really want is the person we were made for, Jesus, and the place we were made for, Heaven. Nothing less can satisfy us.[8]

According to the Bible, humans were created to live with God. Adam and Eve were put in the Garden of Eden so they could do just that (Genesis 2). However, because of their disobedience, the first couple was expelled from their natural home and exiled from God (Genesis 3). They found themselves living on a planet gone awry. So do we.

The Bible gives us a clear allegorical picture of our situation in the story of the Israelites in Egypt. That famous tale starts with God promising Abraham that his descendents would be a great nation and be placed in a country of their own, the land of Canaan (Genesis 12:2-7). The fulfill-ment of that vow seemed to be in jeopardy when Abraham's grandson Jacob was forced to move the entire family to Egypt because of famine (Genesis 41-47). For the next 400 years, the Israelites (the children of Israel, Abraham's grandson) lived in a land that was not their home. So do we. Just as the Israelites were aliens and strangers on foreign soil, longing for the country they were meant to live in, we are aliens and strangers on this fallen planet, longing for our true home. We will not be satisfied until we get there.

Of course that is not the full story. After all, if the main problem the Israelites faced was being away from home, they simply could have packed up and moved. However, they couldn't do that because they were slaves. As the number of Israelites grew over the years, successive rulers of Egypt forced them into slavery to keep them from becoming a threat (Exodus 1:8-11). The Israelites couldn't leave because they didn't have the power to overthrow the oppressive ruler. They needed help.

The Bible tells us that this is the human predicament as well. Not only is this planet not our home, but we are slaves to Satan. When Adam and Eve rebelled, the devil took control. Satan is called the prince of this world (John 12:31, 14:30, 16:11), the god of this age (2 Corinthians 4:4), the ruler of the kingdom of the air (Ephesians 2:2), and the ruler of darkness (Ephesians 6:12). During the temptation of Christ in the desert, Satan showed Jesus "all the king-doms of the world" and said to him, "I will give you all their authority and splendor, for it has been given to me, and I can give it to anyone I want to" (Luke 4:6). Scripture is clear that Satan has authority over this planet.

It is also clear that we are slaves in his evil kingdom. The Apostle Paul writes that everyone is "sold as a slave to sin" (Romans 7:14), a sentiment echoed by Jesus in John 8:34: "I tell you the truth, everyone who sins is a slave to sin." Paul also argues that "when you offer yourselves to someone you obey him as slaves, you are slaves to the one whom you obey – whether you are slaves to sin, which leads to death, or to obedience, which leads to righteousness (Romans 6:16). In a letter to Timothy, Paul tells his apprentice that the ungodly must be instructed "in the hope that that God will grant them repentance leading them to a knowledge of the truth, and that they will come to their senses and escape from the trap of the devil, who has taken them captive to do his will" (2 Timothy 2:25b-26).

So the allegorical picture of our situation looks like this: Egypt is Earth, the Egyptian ruler, Pharaoh, is Satan and the Promised Land, Canaan, is Heaven. Just like the Israelites, we find ourselves living as slaves in a foreign land; and just like the Israelites, we don't seem to have the power or ability to find our way home. This is why we are not content.

Although our situation is dire, understanding the problem should actually bring some sense of relief to all those who have been struggling to find happiness. G.K. Chesterton writes how glad he was to discover the horrible truth of his predicament.

> According to Christianity, we [are] the survivors of a wreck, the crew of a golden ship that had gone down before the beginning of the world....
>
> I had often called myself an optimist, to avoid the too evident blasphemy of pessimism. But all the optimism of the age had been false and disheartening for this reason, that it had always been trying to prove that we fit in to the world. The Christian optimism is based on the fact that we do *not* fit in to the world. I had tried to be happy by telling myself that man is an animal, like any other which sought its meat from God. But now I really was happy, for I had learnt

that man is a monstrosity. I had been right in feeling all things as odd, for I myself was at once worse and better than all things. The optimist's pleasure was prosaic, for it dwelt on the naturalness of everything; the Christian pleasure was poetic, for it dwelt on the unnaturalness of everything in the light of the supernatural. The modern philosopher had told me again and again that I was in the right place, and I had still felt depressed even in acquiescence. But I had heard that I was in the *wrong* place, and my soul sang for joy, like a bird in spring. The knowledge found out and illuminated forgotten chambers in the dark house of infancy. I knew now why grass had always seemed to me as queer as the green beard of a giant, and why I could feel homesick at home.[9]

Chesterton found great joy at realizing what he had been missing, and I think we should, too. However, as nice as it is to learn what our problem is, knowing the truth about our predicament will still lead to despair if there is not a solution to this mess. Is there any hope? Is there a way home? Yes. That is what this book is about.

The Gospel According to Exodus

The Israelites called out to God and asked Him to rescue them from their suffering (Exodus 2:23). In response, he enacted the great drama of redemption that we now know as the story of the Exodus. As I will explain, that story can be ours as well.

The historical account of the Israelites is not just an allegory in describing living in slavery to a foreign tyrant. It also describes salvation from that situation. The extraordinary tale of the Israelites' escape from slavery and journey to the Promised Land is a metaphorical roadmap of the path to Heaven. The story of their redemption is meant to instruct us about what is necessary for our redemption. By learning how the Israelites arrived (or failed to arrive) at their home, we can learn how to reach ours.

Before we turn to the details of that saga, let me briefly describe the path this book will take. I will compare God's plan of salvation for us with that of his plan for the sojourning Israelites in each of three stages: the escape from Egypt, the wilderness wanderings and the entry into the Promised Land.

In Part 1, we will talk about what God did to get the slaves out of Egypt. First he sent a unique man to lead them. Then he demonstrated his power and authority over the gods of Egypt through many signs and wonders. Finally, he poured out his wrath on the land by sending the angel of death to kill all the firstborn. However, those who followed God's Passover directions were saved from destruction as he allowed for this punishment to fall on a lamb instead. We will see how Jesus fulfilled the events of that story during his ministry on earth so that we might be set free and escape slavery to sin and Satan.

After being set free from Egypt, the Children of Israel wandered for years in the wilderness before settling in the Promised Land. We will discuss several episodes from this period in Part 2, examining what God's path for the Israelites teaches about his path for us. Salvation is not a one-time event. Nor is it easy. The road to Heaven is a long and marked with very rough terrain. The Israelite's wilderness wanderings teach many valuable lessons about the nature of that expedition.

The third and final section is about what it takes to actually enter into the Promised Land. Many Israelites made it out of Egypt and across all or most of the wilderness only to fail before entering Canaan. Making it to Heaven requires persevering all the way to the end. We will examine what the

Israelites did wrong and offer some principles to implement so as to avoid their mistakes.

This book is not a commentary on Exodus. It does not provide comprehensive or exhaustive exegesis of any particular passages. I am not going to plumb the depths of every verse of scripture or extract every principle out of any single part of the story. I simply want to help us view more clearly the big picture of redemption as it is portrayed in the Exodus story.

Sometimes people talk as if God's plan of salvation is an engineering project or a business transaction. Using dry theological terms, they make redemption sound like a stale and impersonal mathematical equation. It is anything but. The way to Heaven is a journey, full of traps and pitfalls and deadly enemies. Indeed, it has much more in common with an action adventure movie than a scientific formula. I want to help us think outside some of those theological boxes. God invites each of us on an incredible adventure. I write this book to offer his insight into how to proceed successfully.

(If you have seen *The Ten Commandments* or attended Sunday School, you are probably at least somewhat familiar with this classic tale, and if not you are in for a treat. I will be summarizing the story and quoting extensively from the biblical text, but no matter how well you know the story, I highly recommend taking the time to read or reread Exodus as a companion to this book.)

PART I

Out of Egypt

Set Free by God

CHAPTER 1

The Deliverer

I am the LORD, and I will bring you out from under the yoke of the Egyptians. I will free you from being slaves to them, and I will redeem you with an outstretched arm and with mighty acts of judgment.

EXODUS 6:6

He has sent me to proclaim freedom for the prisoners and recovery of sight for the blind, to release the oppressed, to proclaim the year of the Lord's favor.

LUKE 4:18-19

In one of the most famous scenes in the original *Star Wars*, the hero of the story breaks into a jail cell holding a beautiful damsel in distress and introduces himself with the words "I'm Luke Skywalker, I'm here to rescue you." The prisoner is not impressed. "You're who?" she asks incredulously. One skinny young farm boy was not who Princess Leia was hoping to liberate her. After all, a battalion of war-hardened soldiers would barely have been sufficient to defeat the Imperial forces holding her captive. What was this kid going to do to help? Was she really supposed to follow him? Could he really be her only way to freedom?

As it turned out, yes. It might have seemed unlikely at the time, but one man did result in Princess Leia's release from bondage and certain death. She did the right thing by placing her trust in him.

Just like Princess Leia, you might have certain expectations about your path to freedom. Perhaps you accept the oft-quoted maxim that there are many ways to Heaven, and each of us can decide for ourselves how to get there. However, as we will learn from the biblical stories of the Exodus and Jesus, it all boils down to following one unlikely man.

Moses

After briefly explaining how the Israelites ended up as slaves, the book of Exodus starts the story of their deliverance by telling about birth of Moses, the one who will lead the Israelites home. We learn that Moses is born in a time when, in an attempt to quell an uprising before it starts, the Pharaoh has ordered all male Jewish babies to be thrown into the Nile (Exodus 1:22). Moses' mother responds bravely, and the result is one of the greatest stories of all time:

> Now a man of the house of Levi married a Levite woman, and she became pregnant and gave birth to a son. When she saw that he was a fine child, she hid him for three months. But when she could hide him no longer, she got a papyrus basket for him and coated it with tar and pitch. Then she placed the child in it and put it among the reeds along the bank of the

Nile. His sister stood at a distance to see what would happen to him.

Then Pharaoh's daughter went down to the Nile to bathe, and her attendants were walking along the river bank. She saw the basket among the reeds and sent her slave girl to get it. She opened it and saw the baby. He was crying, and she felt sorry for him. "This is one of the Hebrew babies," she said.

Then his sister asked Pharaoh's daughter, "Shall I go and get one of the Hebrew women to nurse the baby for you?"

"Yes, go," she answered. And the girl went and got the baby's mother. Pharaoh's daughter said to her, "Take this baby and nurse him for me, and I will pay you." So the woman took the baby and nursed him. When the child grew older, she took him to Pharaoh's daughter and he became her son. She named him Moses, saying, "I drew him out of the water." (Exodus 2:1-10)

Moses grew up as royalty, the son of the Pharaoh. However, he never forgot his Hebrew identity, and one day he killed an Egyptian who was beating an Israelite slave. When his action became known, Moses was forced to flee the palace and live in exile in Midian (Exodus 2:11-15). There he lived for the next 40 years until God called to him from the burning bush and told him to go back and lead the Hebrews out of slavery (Exodus 3).

We'll get to Moses' return to Egypt in the next chapter, but I want to pause here and emphasize the fact that God's plan to rescue the Hebrews involved sending a man. Conceivably God could have used any number of means to set his people free, but he chose to send a single man. He did this, I believe, to point us toward, and help us understand, the man he would later send to rescue all of humanity from the clutches of Satan. Moses was a type of Christ. As we grasp Moses' role in leading the Israelites out of slavery, we better comprehend what Jesus has done and is doing for us.

Similarities Between Moses and Jesus

The first similarity between Moses and Jesus involves the circumstances of their birth. Moses was born into an oppressed people living under an evil tyrant who tried to have him killed. So was Jesus. Just like the Pharaoh centuries before him, King Herod was concerned about someone rising up to take his throne (Matthew 2:3-6). He heard that a "King of the Jews" had been born and, in order to quell an uprising before it started, he ordered that all Hebrew babies 2 years old and younger be killed (Matthew 2:16). Jesus' parents fled to Egypt, where they stayed until Herod died (Matthew 2:14-15).

Another aspect of Moses' life that points toward Jesus is the fact that he gave up his position of honor and privilege to identify with the people he loved. Moses was a powerful prince, but he became a nobody, a shepherd herding flocks in the middle of nowhere. The writer of Hebrews describes his action this way: "By faith Moses, when he had grown up, refused to be known as the son of Pharaoh's daughter. He chose to be mistreated along with the people of God rather than to enjoy the pleasures of sin for a short time" (Hebrews 11:24-25).

In the same spirit as Moses, Jesus gave up his position in Heaven to identify with the people he loved and become a man. Paul portrays Jesus in these glowing terms: "Who, being in very nature God, did not consider equality with God something to be grasped, but made himself nothing, taking the very nature of a servant, being made in human like-ness. And being found in appearance as a man, he humbled himself and became obedient to death — even death on a cross!" (Philippians 2:6-8).

Here is another similarity: when Moses came to lead his people, most didn't welcome him with open arms. Pharaoh responded to Moses' first demand to let the people go by making their work even harder, which resulted in the Hebrews cursing Moses for bringing more trouble on them.

> The Israelite foremen realized they were in trouble when they were told, "You are not to reduce the number of bricks required of you for each day." When they left Pharaoh, they found Moses and Aaron waiting to meet them, and they said, "May the LORD look upon you and judge you! You have made us a stench to Pharaoh and his officials and have put a sword in their hand to kill us." (Exodus 5:19-21)

In the same way, Jesus was "despised and rejected by men, a man of sorrows, and familiar with suffering. Like one from whom men hide their faces he was despised, and we esteemed him not" (Isaiah 53:3). John explains that "he came to that which was his own, but his own did not receive him" (John 1:11). Jesus came to set humanity free, but most people weren't interested. Rather than follow, they called for his crucifixion.

Belonging to Two Families

Moses and Jesus had remarkably similar experiences that should make us ponder the link between the two men. However, I believe the strongest illustrative parallel between Moses and Jesus is the unique family ties that each possessed. Both Moses and Jesus were members of two families, one royal and one common, and these multiple connections were necessary to complete their redemptive mission.

As we learned, Moses was born a Jew but was adopted into the Egyptian ruling family. As a Hebrew he was able to relate to the people and exercise the authority necessary to lead them; it seems unlikely they would have followed a non-Israelite. On the other hand, as a son of the Pharaoh, Moses was granted the access necessary to enter the court and demand the slaves' release. It seems unlikely that he would have been able to do this if he was not family. Moses needed to be both an Egyptian royal and a Jew to accomplish his task.

In the same way, Jesus is a man but is also God. He was born to Mary in Bethlehem, but at the same time has always existed as part of the Godhead (John 1:1). As a member of the human family, he is able to relate to us and exercise the necessary authority to lead us home. As the Son of God, Jesus has access to the very throne room of God, so that he might make intercession for us (Romans 8:34). The fact that he was both God and man was and is absolutely essential to his goal.

God providentially placed Moses in the Pharaoh's family so, when the time was right, he would have access to the seat of power and secure the Jews' release. In this way, God illustrated what would later occur with Jesus. God did a similar thing later in Israel's history with a young lady named Esther. Esther was also a type of Jesus in that she, too, was a member of two families who interceded with the king to save her people.

I won't tell the whole story here, but Esther was a Jewish girl who won a contest and became King Xerxes' queen (Esther 1, 2). Xerxes did not know at the time that Esther was Jewish, so when Haman, a trusted nobleman close to the king, devised a plot to kill all the Jews in the land, Xerxes went along with it (Esther 3:6-15). Esther's cousin Mordecai convinced her that she had to do something to stop the annihilation of her people, and Esther bravely went before the king to intercede on their behalf (Esther 4:1-5:2). There are many more interesting twists and turns within the biblical account, but the bottom line is that Esther's plea was successful and the Jews were saved (Esther 5:3-9:17). Just as he had done with Moses, God providentially placed Esther in the royal family so she could have access to the seat of power when that became necessary to save the Israelites. Both Moses and Esther are people who illuminate Jesus, the human who has the membership in the divine royal family that is necessary to save us.

One Redeemer

Just as God sent one man, Moses, to lead the Israelites out of slavery, God sent one man, Jesus, to lead humanity out of slavery. Jesus came to Earth to deliver us from Satan and to lead us across the wilderness to the Promised Land. His self-professed mission was a fulfillment of Isaiah 61:1: "The Spirit of the Lord is on me, because he has anointed me to preach good news to the poor. He has sent me to proclaim freedom for the prisoners and recovery of sight for the blind, to release the oppressed, to proclaim the year of the Lord's favor" (Luke 4:18-19). In one of his more famous lines, Jesus summed up the reason that people should hold to his teaching: "Then you will know the truth, and the truth will set you free" (John 8:32).

We need to look to Jesus for our deliverance in the same way that the Israelites looked to Moses, because just as Moses fulfilled a unique role, Jesus fills a unique role. Just as Moses was the only one called and equipped by God to lead the people home, Jesus is the only one able to lead us home.

The Israelites could have tried to find some other way out of Egypt, but God's plan allowed for only one way: behind Moses. Humanity continues to try to travel many paths to God, but God's plan allows for only one way: behind Jesus. When Jesus came and declared the way of redemption, he didn't say, "Find your own path" or "Any road will do," he said, "Follow me" (Mark 1:14-20; 2:13-14, for example) and "I am the way and the truth and the life. No one comes to the Father except through me" (John 14:6). Falling in line behind Jesus is the first step on the journey home.

"But why should we trust that Jesus knows the way?" you might ask. "What gives him the right to call us to follow?" To that we now turn.

CHAPTER 2

Who Is This Man?

Pharaoh said, "Who is the LORD, that I should obey him and let Israel go?"

EXODUS 5:2

They were terrified and asked each other, "Who is this? Even the wind and the waves obey him!"

MARK 4:42

Moses' first meeting with the Pharaoh didn't go very well. When Moses demanded the release of the slaves, the Egyptian ruler scoffed at the notion by asking, "Who is the LORD, that I should obey him and let Israel go?" (Exodus 5:2). This was a rhetorical question. Pharaoh was not asking Moses for a treatise on the nature of his god. He was making a statement about the perceived authority of that god. "On whose authority are you asking me to do this, Moses? Who is this LORD of yours that he would order me around? Does he really think he is so high on the hierarchy of divine powers that he can demand something of me, the Pharaoh? How foolish."

Pharaoh denied Moses' request because he did not believe the LORD had the authority to ask it. While he didn't necessarily deny the existence of Moses' god, by not freeing the slaves Pharaoh made a point about how little authority he thought the LORD possessed. The plagues that followed were God's answer to Pharaoh's question. "You want to know who I am, Pharaoh? You want to know how much authority, I have? Let me show you."

Establishing Identity Through Exercise of Authority

We all understand what it means to live within a hierarchical authority. If we have any experience with schools, businesses, the government or the armed forces, for example, we know how authority works. Authority is the power to make decisions and see those decisions implemented. People operate within hierarchical structures according to varying degrees of authority.

A friend of mine manages a retail store. He has the authority to hire and fire everyone who works in his store. He also sets their work schedules and assigns their duties. He has authority to make these decisions and see them implemented. However, other decisions are not his to make. For example, he does not have the authority to decide where his store is located or how much the store will charge for products. Those decisions are made by someone higher in the chain of command, someone with more authority.

In the same way, army generals get to decide which divisions of troops to send into battle, but they do not get to decide which country to attack. School teachers have the authority to decide which day an assignment will be due or a test will be taken, but they do not get to decide what days school will be in session. Generals and teachers wield a certain amount of authority, but they also have to submit to a certain amount of authority.

Within this context, let's suppose that I am working as a cashier at my friend's store, and someone I don't know walks in and tells me to pack my bags because the store is closing down. The first thing I would think is "Who are you? Can you fire me? Do you have that authority?"

Now let's suppose that the person doesn't present any credentials or stand around to chat. He just tells me what to do and proceeds through the store. I decide that he must be delusional and that I will ignore his directives and just keep working. I operate as if he does not have the authority he was claiming. However, I soon see something that makes me question my decision. My friend, the store manager, has been talking to the man and is now in the process of cleaning out his office. Realizing that the man who talked to me must have the authority he was claiming when he ordered me to leave, I pack up and go.

Although I had never met this person and didn't see any standard forms of identification, I now realize that if the man has, in fact, the authority to fire the store manager, he certainly has the authority to fire me. By the simple exercise of his authority, his ability to make a decision and see it implemented, I can tell that this person is someone very high up in the company, perhaps even the president or owner. I have deduced from his exercise of authority who this person is.

Using the same methods, we can often answer the question, "Who is this person?" by examining how much authority they wield. We can figure out a person's identity, or at least narrow the possibilities down to a few, by seeing what decisions they make and are able to see implemented. If there are only five people in the company with the authority to close stores and fire general managers, then I can safely assume that the person who came to my store was one of those five.

Sometimes we can even narrow the possibilities down to one. For example, there is only one person on the planet with the authority to launch U.S. nuclear weapons: the president. If I found myself witnessing the nuclear "football," (the suitcase containing the nuclear launch codes that never leaves the president's side) being opened and certified by secret service men and then I saw a man push the launch button, because there is only one man with the authority to do that, I could safely assume that that man was the president. I realize it is unlikely that [1] a person wouldn't recognize the president and [2] that person would be in a place to witness nuclear weapons being launched, but I hope you get the point: it is possible to deduce the identity of people by their exercise of authority.

The Authority of the LORD

Now let's return to Exodus. Not only did the Pharaoh not submit to orders from God, he mocked him. This is like me laughing in the face of the guy who told me the store was closing and saying to him with derision, "And who do you think you are, the big boss man?" Pharaoh asks, "Who is the LORD?" in just that mocking tone, it seems. Whatever his tone, Pharaoh is certainly saying that the LORD is not someone he needs to listen to. However, just like me, Pharaoh gets an answer he didn't expect. God goes on to display an exercise of authority that is much more powerful than making the store manager pack up his office. It will leave the Pharaoh wishing he had never been so snide and self-assured.

The first evidence of God's authority involved sticks and snakes. Moses and Aaron appeared before Pharaoh and were asked for a miracle to support their claims. Aaron threw his staff on the floor, and it turned into a snake (Exodus 7:8-10). Unimpressed, Pharaoh summoned his magicians and they did the same thing (Exodus 7:11). However, something very interesting happened next. Aaron's staff swallowed up the other staffs. This is of critical importance as it prefigures what is about to happen in the story. With this action, God was saying to Pharaoh, "I have greater power and authority than any of the gods and magicians of Egypt." It was but a small taste of what was to come. Although there is not a scholarly consensus on what specific Egyptian god each of the 10 plagues was intended to defeat, it is generally agreed that they were indeed meant to show that the gods of Egypt had less power and authority than the LORD, the god of Israel (Exodus 12:12; Numbers 33:4). By the end of the plagues, the answer to the question "Who is the LORD?" would be clear. He is the one who has ultimate authority on Heaven and Earth.

The demonstration began in earnest with the first plague.

> The LORD said to Moses, "Tell Aaron, 'Take your staff and stretch out your hand over the waters of Egypt – over the streams and canals, over the ponds and all the reservoirs' – and they will turn to blood. Blood will be everywhere in Egypt, even in the wooden buckets and stone jars." Moses and Aaron did just as the LORD had commanded. He raised his staff in the presence of Pharaoh and his officials and struck the water of the Nile, and all the water was changed into blood. The fish in the Nile died, and the river smelled so bad that the Egyptians could not drink its water. Blood was everywhere in Egypt. (Exodus 7:19-21)

The Nile River was viewed as the source of life of Egypt. It was understood to determine the welfare of the people by providing necessary water for man, animals and crops.

Without the Nile, Egypt was uninhabitable. By getting the river to obey his commands, God showed that he had authority over the river and that the God of Moses had more control over the life of the people than the Nile.

Interestingly, the Egyptian magicians were able to perform the same miracle (Exodus 7:22). At this point in the story it seems that, although the Nile and the gods associated with it could no longer be considered the highest authority in Egypt, some other gods of Egypt were still in contention. Perhaps banking on one of those gods to ultimately win the battle, Pharaoh did not relent and release the Israelites.

The next plague left the land absolutely teeming with frogs (Exodus 8:1-5). Again the magicians were able to duplicate the feat (Exodus 8:7). However, it seems they were unable to make the frogs go away, and the Pharaoh was forced to ask Moses and Aaron to appeal to their god to remove them (Exodus 8:8), which they did (Exodus 8:9-14). By removing the frogs, the LORD distinguished himself a bit further from the gods of Egypt by showing their lack of authority to undo what they had started.

That distinction became a little clearer in the following plague. Aaron stretched out his staff, and the dust became gnats (Exodus 9:16-17). When the magicians tried to reproduce the plague, they could not (Exodus 9:18). Now God was starting to make crystal clear who had the authority in this situation. He was able to make and implement decisions that no one else could. He was emphatically answering the question "Who is this god, the LORD?" Even the Pharaoh's magicians had the correct answer by this time and implored the ruler to let the people go, but he would not listen (Exodus 8:19).

Having shown that he had greater authority than the gods of Egypt, God used the rest of the plagues to demonstrate just how far this authority extended and to clarify that, indeed, it is the LORD, God of Israel who wielded it. He wanted to make absolutely clear to Egypt, the Israelites and the world that the god who chose Israel to be his people is Lord of Lords, the Almighty, the One True God. He did this by sending progressively more damaging plagues that only affected the Egyptians and left the Israelites unharmed.

For example, God next sent swarms of flies to cover everything in Egypt except the land of Goshen, where the Israelites lived (Exodus 8:20-23). This was intended to demonstrate not only that he had the prerogative to send plagues, but that he could define their boundaries. There could be no mistaking this plague for a natural occurrence, as flies would not stop at political borders, nor could there be any doubt about with whom this God was siding.

The subsequent plague resulted in the death of Egyptian cattle, apparently through some type of disease. However, none of the Israelite cattle were harmed (Exodus 9:1-6). Then came the boils, which affected not just the animals but all the Egyptian people as well (Exodus 9:8-12). After that, hail rained down, which left Egypt in such bad condition that even Pharaoh's officials told him to let the Israelites go (Exodus 10:7). Pharaoh refused, so God sent locusts that devoured everything in the land (Exodus 10:13-15). The ninth plague was darkness. This was not just twilight or an overly cloudy day, but "darkness that [could] be felt" (Exodus 10:21). Many scholars believe this was to demonstrate that God's authority extended even beyond that of the highest deity in Egypt, the sun god Ra.

We will talk about the final plague and the Passover in the next chapter. For now let's review the meaning of the first nine plagues and reiterate the message that God was sending to the world. Then we will examine how Jesus fulfills this story and presents us with the same message.

Pharaoh started the proceedings by asking "Who is the LORD? Does he have authority to stake a claim to my workforce?" The answer was unequivocal: the god of the

Israelites this is the ultimate god, the god over all gods. God emphatically demonstrated that he had the right to decide that his people should be free and that he had the power to see that freedom accomplished. God revealed who he was through the exercise of his authority over all the powers that held the Israelites in bondage.

The Authority of Jesus

Jesus claimed to be our redeemer. As we noted in Chapter 1, his self-professed mission was to set the captives free (Luke 4:18-19; John 8:32) and his message was a call to "Follow me." On what basis should we believe this claim and heed this call? Does Jesus have the authority to defeat the powers that bind us and the right to demand our allegiance? Absolutely.

When Jesus came to earth, he made the same claims as the God of the Israelites and faced the same questions about his authority to make such claims. He also demonstrated his authority and answered his skeptics in exactly the same way. In his teachings and actions, Jesus made clear that he was the one who had the authority to call us from bondage and to free us from the penalty and power of sin and Satan. In other words, he claimed to have the right to decide that we could be free and he demonstrated the power to see that decision realized.

For example, in Mark 2:5, Jesus says to a paralytic, "Son, your sins are forgiven." Since everyone in the culture understood that only God can forgive sins, this was a clear assertion of ultimate authority. It quickly evoked skepticism: "Now some teachers of the law were sitting there, thinking to themselves, 'Why does this fellow talk like that? He's blaspheming! Who can forgive sins but God alone?'"(Mark 2:6-7).

"Who does this guy think he is?" the religious leaders were asking, "Almighty God?" Just as Pharaoh had mocked the claims of Moses' God, these men were mocking the claims of Jesus. Just as Pharaoh asserted that the God of Moses had no authority to free the Jews from his control, the religious leaders were saying that Jesus had no right to free the sinners from Satan's control. And just as the God of Moses backed up his claim with a demonstration of his power and authority, Jesus did exactly the same thing by performing a miracle.

> Immediately Jesus knew in his spirit that this was what they were thinking in their hearts, and he said to them, "Why are you thinking these things? Which is easier: to say to the paralytic, 'Your sins are forgiven,' or to say, 'get up, take your mat and walk'? But that you may know that the Son of Man has authority on earth to forgive sins... ." He said to the paralytic, "I tell you, get up, take your mat and go home." He got up, took his mat and walked out in full view of them all. This amazed everyone and they praised God, saying, "We have never seen anything like this!" (Mark 2:8-12)

The plagues showed Pharaoh that the God of Israel did indeed have authority to call his people to freedom. By healing the paralytic, Jesus showed the teachers of the law that he had authority to forgive sins. In healing the paralytic, he was answering the question, "Who is this man?" Of course, authority over physical illness was not the only area of life over which Jesus demonstrated his power. Just as God used 10 plagues to show that his authority extended over every aspect of the universe and all the gods of Egypt, Jesus did a variety of signs and wonders to show the extent of his authority. He drove out demons, calmed storms, produced miraculous amounts of food and raised the dead, among other things. Each incident was intended to further answer the question, "Who is this man?" For example, notice the response of the crowds in the following passage from Luke.

> In the synagogue there was a man possessed by a demon, an evil spirit. He cried out at the top of his voice, "Ha! What do you want with us, Jesus of Nazareth? Have you come to destroy us? I know who you are—the Holy One of God!"
>
> "Be quiet!" Jesus said sternly. "Come out of him!" Then the demon threw the man down before them all and came out without injuring him.
>
> All the people were amazed and said to each other, "What is this teaching? With authority and power he gives orders to evil spirits and they come out!" And the news about him spread throughout the surrounding area. (Luke 4:33-37)

Jesus' disciples reacted in a similar fashion when he calmed the sea.

> That day when evening came, he said to his disciples, "Let us go over to the other side." Leaving the crowd behind, they took him along, just as he was, in the boat. There were also other boats with him. A furious squall came up, and the waves broke over the boat, so that it was nearly swamped. Jesus was in the stern, sleeping on a cushion. The disciples woke him and said to him, "Teacher, don't you care if we drown?"
>
> He got up, rebuked the wind and said to the waves, "Quiet! Be still!" Then the wind died down and it was completely calm.

He said to his disciples, "Why are you so afraid? Do you still have no faith?"

They were terrified and asked each other, "Who is this? Even the wind and the waves obey him!" (Mark 4:35-41)

Everyone had the same question: "Who is this man?" They were left with only one reasonable answer: Jesus is the one with all authority, he is the ruler over all, he is God. The Pharisees asked the question, "Who can forgive sins but God alone?" The answer is nobody. Only Almighty God has the authority to forgive sins. By forgiving sins Jesus claimed to be God. Then he gave support to his claim by answering several other questions, such as, "Who can cast out demons but God alone?" and, "Who can tell the wind and waves what to do but God alone?" Again, the answer is "Nobody." Yet Jesus did those things, too. Through his miraculous work Jesus made the case that he was God, and as such he did have the authority to call his people to freedom.

The Apostle John structured his Gospel around seven major miracles of Jesus. Near the end of the book he explains why: "Jesus did many other miraculous signs in the presence of his disciples, which are not recorded in this book. But these are written that you may believe that Jesus is the Christ, the Son of God, and that by believing you may have life in his name" (John 20:30-31).

Just as God gave Pharaoh and the Israelites good reasons to believe that he had all authority to call the Israelites out of slavery to Pharaoh, Jesus gave us good reasons to believe that he has the authority to call us out of slavery to sin and Satan. Jesus didn't just show up and say, "Trust me" without giving us good reasons to do so. Following him is not a blind leap of irrational faith. When Jesus says that he knows the way to the Promised Land (John 14:1-6), our only reasonable response is to follow him.

CHAPTER 3

Under the Blood of the Lamb

The blood will be a sign for you on the houses where you are; and when I see the blood, I will pass over you. No destructive plague will touch you when I strike Egypt.

EXODUS 12:13

For you know that it was not with perishable things such as silver or gold that you were redeemed from the empty way of life handed down to you from your forefathers, but with the precious blood of Christ, a lamb without blemish or defect.

1 PETER 1:18-19

Through the first nine plagues, the LORD, god of Israel had clearly established his identity as god of gods and possessor of all authority. However, the Children of Israel were still not released. Even after all the suffering his kingdom had faced, Pharaoh still would not let the Hebrews go (Exodus 10:27). However, God promised Moses that the tenth plague would result in their freedom (Exodus 11:1), so Moses explained the situation to Pharaoh.

> Moses said, "This is what the LORD says: 'About midnight I will go throughout Egypt. Every first-born son in Egypt will die, from the firstborn son of Pharaoh, who sits on the throne, to the firstborn son of the slave girl, who is at her hand mill, and all the firstborn of the cattle as well. There will be loud wailing throughout Egypt – worse than there has ever been or ever will be again. But among the Israelites not a dog will bark at any man or animal.' Then you will know that the LORD makes a distinction between Egypt and Israel. All these officials of yours will come to me, bowing down before me and saying, 'Go, you and all the people who follow you!' After that I will leave." Then Moses, hot with anger, left Pharaoh. (Exodus 11:4-8)

You might wonder why God had to go to such lengths. After all, isn't killing all the firstborn in the land a little harsh, even for someone as stubborn as the Pharaoh? Here it is important to understand that the plagues were not just signs of God's authority. The plagues were also acts of justice. God used the plagues to punish Egypt for its rebellion against him and worship of other gods. God had explained this to Moses before the plagues started: "Therefore, say to the Israelites: 'I am the LORD, and I will bring you out from under the yoke of the Egyptians. I will free you from being slaves to them, and I will redeem you with an outstretched arm and with mighty acts of judgment.'" (Exodus 6:6). God then reiterated this theme before the final plague. "On that same night I will pass through Egypt and strike down every first-born—both men and animals—and I will bring judgment on all the gods of Egypt. I am the LORD" (Exodus 12:12).

As the Psalmist explains, God is just in dealing with nations. Rebellious people reap what they sow.

> The nations have fallen into the pit they have dug; their feet are caught in the net they have hidden.
>
> The LORD is known by his justice; the wicked are ensnared by the work of their hands.
>
> The wicked return to the grave, all the nations that forget God.
>
> But the needy will not always be forgotten, nor the hope of the afflicted ever perish.
>
> Arise, O LORD, let not man triumph; let the nations be judged in your presence.
>
> Strike them with terror, O LORD; let the nations know they are but men. (Psalm 9:15-20)

The wages of sin is death (Romans 6:23). Through the death of the firstborn, God was bringing justice on Egypt for their sins. But, you might ask, what about the sins of the rest of the people? Why just the firstborn? And what about the sins of Israel? Were they any different in their rejection of God? No. This is where the symbolic and allegorical nature of the Exodus story really comes into play.

Two aspects of the final plague are very interesting. First, God limited the punishment to the firstborn. Though he is not the only one that is guilty, the firstborn of every family pays the penalty for everyone else. God could have simply wiped out the entire population and been justified. However, he limited the punishment to a symbolic group. Second, God gave a way for even that group to escape his wrath. He gave the people the option of having their punishment paid by a lamb. Rather than the firstborn of a family paying the price for everyone, a young sheep would die in his place. God explained to Moses how it would work.

The LORD said to Moses and Aaron in Egypt, "This month is to be for you the first month, the first month of your year. Tell the whole community of Israel that on the tenth day of this month each man is to take a lamb for his family, one for each household. If any household is too small for a whole lamb, they must share one with their nearest neighbor, having taken into account the number of people there are. You are to determine the amount of lamb needed in accordance with what each person will eat. The animals you choose must be year-old males without defect, and you may take them from the sheep or the goats. Take care of them until the fourteenth day of the month, when all the people of the community of Israel must slaughter them at twilight. Then they are to take some of the blood and put it on the sides and tops of the doorframes of the houses where they eat the lambs. That same night they are to eat the meat roasted over the fire, along with bitter herbs, and bread made without yeast. Do not eat the meat raw or cooked in water, but roast it over the fire – head, legs and inner parts. Do not leave any of it till morning; if some is left till morning, you must burn it. This is how you are to eat it: with your cloak tucked into your belt, your sandals on your feet and your staff in your hand. Eat it in haste; it is the LORD's Passover.

"On that same night I will pass through Egypt and strike down every firstborn – both men and animals – and I will bring judgment on all the gods of Egypt.

I am the LORD. The blood will be a sign for you on the houses where you are; and when I see the blood, I will pass over you. No destructive plague will touch you when I strike Egypt." (Exodus 12:1-13)

By placing the blood on the doorframe, those that followed God's plan escaped judgment. Sin still resulted in death, but rather than everyone's death, or even the death of the first-born, the penalty for this group's sin was paid by the death of a lamb.

God then gave Moses instructions for the continual remembrance of this event. I think it is important to read this part in its entirety so that we may see how clearly Jesus fits into the story.

"This is a day you are to commemorate; for the generations to come you shall celebrate it as a festival to the LORD – a lasting ordinance. For seven days you are to eat bread made without yeast. On the first day remove the yeast from your houses, for whoever eats anything with yeast in it from the first day through the seventh must be cut off from Israel. On the first day hold a sacred assembly, and another one on the seventh day. Do no work at all on these days, except to prepare food for everyone to eat – that is all you may do.

"Celebrate the Feast of Unleavened Bread, because it was on this very day that I brought your divisions out of Egypt. Celebrate this day as a lasting ordinance for the generations to come. In the first month you are to eat bread made without yeast, from the evening of the fourteenth day until the evening of the twenty-first day. For seven days no yeast is to be found in your houses. And whoever eats anything with yeast in it must be cut off from the community of Israel, whether he is an alien or native-born. Eat nothing made with yeast. Wherever you live, you must eat unleavened bread."

Then Moses summoned all the elders of Israel and said to them, "Go at once and select the animals for your families and slaughter the Passover lamb. Take a bunch of hyssop, dip it into the blood in the basin and put some of the blood on the top and on both sides of the doorframe. Not one of you shall go out the door of his house until morning. When the LORD goes through the land to strike down the Egyptians, he will see the blood on the top and sides of the door-frame and will pass over that doorway, and he will not permit the destroyer to enter your houses and strike you down.

"Obey these instructions as a lasting ordinance for you and your descendants. When you enter the land that the LORD will give you as he promised, observe this ceremony. And when your children ask you, 'What does this ceremony mean to you?' then tell them, 'It is the Passover sacrifice to the LORD, who passed over the houses of the Israelites in Egypt and spared our homes when he struck down the Egyptians.'" Then the people bowed down and worshiped. The Israelites did just what the LORD commanded Moses and Aaron. (Exodus 12:14-28)

Then the final plague and the Passover occurred, just as God said it would, and the people left Egypt.

At midnight the LORD struck down all the firstborn in Egypt, from the firstborn of Pharaoh, who sat on the throne, to the firstborn of the prisoner, who was in the dungeon, and the firstborn of all the livestock as well. Pharaoh and all his officials and all the Egyptians got up during the night, and there was loud wailing in Egypt, for there was not a house without someone dead.

During the night Pharaoh summoned Moses and Aaron and said, "Up! Leave my people, you and the Israelites! Go, worship the LORD as you have requested. Take your flocks and herds, as you have said, and go. And also bless me."

The Egyptians urged the people to hurry and leave the country. "For otherwise," they said, "we will all die!" So the people took their dough before the yeast was added, and carried it on their shoulders in kneading troughs wrapped in clothing. The Israelites did as Moses instructed and asked the Egyptians for articles of silver and gold and for clothing. The LORD had made the Egyptians favorably disposed toward the people, and they gave them what they asked for; so they plundered the Egyptians.

The Israelites journeyed from Rameses to Succoth. There were about six hundred thousand men on foot, besides women and children. Many other people went up with them, as well as large droves of live-stock, both flocks and herds. (Exodus 12:29-38)

Jesus the Lamb

So the way out of Egypt went directly under the blood of the lamb. Only those who trusted God and placed the blood over their doors were able to escape his wrath. In exactly the same fashion, the way to our Promised Land goes directly under the blood of the lamb. Of course for us the lamb is Jesus. He is the one who takes our punishment upon himself. He is the firstborn of God, the pure and spotless one who took the wrath of God on himself when he died on the cross. Because of Jesus we are able to escape Satan's clutches.

The connection between Jesus and the Passover lamb is abundantly clear in scripture. For example, John the Baptist's first words when he saw Jesus were, "Look, the Lamb of God, who takes away the sin of the world!" (John 1:29), a reference he used the next day as well (John 1:36). Paul explicitly calls Christ "our Passover lamb" (1 Corinthians 5:7), and Peter explains why we should live holy lives: "For you know that it was not with perishable things such as silver or gold that you were redeemed from the empty way of life handed down to you from your forefathers, but with the precious blood of Christ, a lamb without blemish or defect" (1 Peter 1:18-19). In addition, the book of Revelation has several references to Jesus being the lamb, including 7:9, 12:11, 13:8, 14:1, 15:3, 17:14, 19:9 and 21:22.

Jesus' connection with the Passover lamb becomes even clearer when we examine the story of his passion. As we read above, God commanded the Israelites to commemorate the Passover with a week-long festival every year. It is no coincidence that Jesus' death occurred exactly during this Passover celebration. As the people commemorated the lamb that was slain for the slaves in Egypt, the fulfillment of that lamb was slain for us. Here are some of the interesting scriptural parallels that make this connection clear.

The fifth day before Passover was lamb selection day, when the families would go and choose a lamb to sacrifice on Passover (the 10th of the month in Exodus 12:3, Passover occurred on the 14th). This is the exact day that Jesus entered Jerusalem during Passion Week, the Lamb of God chosen before the foundation of the world (John 12:12-13, Revelation 13:8).

The Passover lamb had to be without defect, pure and spotless (Exodus 12:5). Jesus lived a perfect life; he was sinless and pure (see 1 Peter 1:19 above). "He committed no sin, and no deceit was found in his mouth" (1 Peter 2:22). According to Paul, "God made him who had no sin to be sin for us, so that in him we might become the righteousness of God" (2 Corinthians 5:21).

During the first Passover, the blood was applied to the doorposts using hyssop, a Mediterranean plant. Hyssop is never mentioned in the Bible outside of the context of purification and forgiveness of sins, and the image of a man lifting a hyssop plant into the air towards a bloody piece of wood would certainly remind a Jew of the Passover. That is exactly what happened in the moment before Jesus' death. A sponge was attached to a hyssop plant, dipped in wine-vinegar, and offered to Jesus (John 19:29).

On the day of the Passover celebration a priest would blow his horn at 3:00 p.m., the moment the Passover lamb was sacrificed. At the sounding of the horn, all the people would pause and contemplate the death of the lamb for their sins. It was at this very moment on Good Friday that Jesus cried out, "It is finished" and gave up his spirit. (Matthew 27:45-50; Mark 15:33-37; Luke 23:44-46; John 19:30).

The Passover lamb was to have none of its bones broken (Exodus 12:46). It was common during crucifixions to break the legs of the victim in order to hasten death. The only way for a person to breathe while hanging on a cross is to push up with their legs, so if the legs are broken, death by asphyxiation comes quickly. During Jesus' crucifixion, soldiers broke the legs of the two men next to Jesus but did not need to do the same to Jesus, as he was already dead (John 19:31-34). John makes the connection between Jesus and the Old

Testament clear by pointing out that this was a fulfillment of prophecy (John 19:35).

All of these "coincidences" are meant to show us that Jesus was our Passover lamb. We deserve to die for our sin, but instead of making us take the punishment ourselves or place it on our firstborn, Jesus took it all. His death allowed us to be set free. Because of the cross we can walk away from slavery.

Before we move on from the Passover, I want to briefly touch on a couple of other stories that illustrate its meaning.

Isaac and the Lamb

So far we have seen Jesus represented in Moses, Esther, the plagues, the firstborn of Egypt and the Passover lamb. However, these are not the only types of Christ in the Bible. In the following story, we see Jesus represented by both Isaac and another sacrificial lamb.

> Some time later God tested Abraham. He said to him, "Abraham!"
>
> "Here I am," he replied.
>
> Then God said, "Take your son, your only son, Isaac, whom you love, and go to the region of Moriah. Sacrifice him there as a burnt offering on one of the mountains I will tell you about."
>
> Early the next morning Abraham got up and saddled his donkey. He took with him two of his servants and his son Isaac. When he had cut enough wood for the burnt offering, he set out for the place God had told him about. On the third day Abraham looked up and saw the place in the distance. He said to his servants, "Stay here with the donkey while I and the boy go

over there. We will worship and then we will come back to you."

Abraham took the wood for the burnt offering and placed it on his son Isaac, and he himself carried the fire and the knife. As the two of them went on together, Isaac spoke up and said to his father Abraham, "Father?"

"Yes, my son?" Abraham replied.

"The fire and wood are here," Isaac said, "but where is the lamb for the burnt offering?"

Abraham answered, "God himself will provide the lamb for the burnt offering, my son." And the two of them went on together.

When they reached the place God had told him about, Abraham built an altar there and arranged the wood on it. He bound his son Isaac and laid him on the altar, on top of the wood. Then he reached out his hand and took the knife to slay his son. But the angel of the LORD called out to him from heaven, "Abraham! Abraham!"

"Here I am," he replied.

"Do not lay a hand on the boy," he said. "Do not do anything to him. Now I know that you fear God, because you have not withheld from me your son, your only son."

Abraham looked up and there in a thicket he saw a ram caught by its horns. He went over and took the ram and sacrificed it as a burnt offering instead of his son. So Abraham called that place The LORD Will Provide. And to this day it is said, "On the mountain of the LORD it will be provided." (Genesis 22:1-14)

Let's start by examining in what ways Isaac is a type of Jesus. Notice the way Isaac is described. God calls him the son Abraham loves. As strange as it may seem, this is the first mention of love in the Bible. The passage speaks of Abraham's love for Isaac, but it also represents God's love for his son, Jesus. Look at how God refers to this story when he offered his son to the world as a sacrifice: "At that time Jesus came from Nazareth in Galilee and was baptized by John in the Jordan. As Jesus was coming up out of the water, he saw heaven being torn open and the Spirit descending on him like a dove. And a voice came from heaven: 'You are my Son, whom I love; with you I am well pleased'" (Mark 1:9-11).

The sacrifice of Isaac was to take place in the region of Moriah. This is commonly referred to as Mount Moriah and is actually a mountain range rather than a single peak. As you may have guessed by now, it was on a hill in this very range that Jesus died on a cross some four thousand years later.

In another interesting and illuminating picture, Isaac actually carried the wood for the sacrifice up the hill on his back. This looks ahead to Jesus' walk to Golgotha, the place of his crucifixion, when he was forced to carry his own cross (John 19:17).

So Isaac the beloved son was presented as a sacrifice in place of the lamb, but at just the right time, God provided a substitute. That substitute was Jesus. God provided his beloved son to actually take the place of the lamb, which no longer needs to be killed. Jesus has accomplished once and for all what the blood of endless lambs could only ever symbolize (Hebrews 10:4, 11): he paid the penalty for our sin.

In the story of Abraham and Isaac, then, Jesus is represented by Isaac and the lamb caught in the thicket. He is the son that is presented for sacrifice, and also the lamb who was actually sacrificed so Isaac could go free. This is another example of a Passover fulfillment. Just as the Passover lamb's blood was spilled so the Hebrews could go free, Jesus' blood was spilled so that we could go free. Praise God!

Peter Set Free from Prison on Passover

It is amazing to consider how many times God has tried to make clear what happened on Passover. Even after Jesus had risen from the dead, God gave us an object lesson in the life of Peter to help us understand it.

It was about this time that King Herod arrested some who belonged to the church, intending to persecute them. He had James, the brother of John, put to death with the sword. When he saw that this pleased the Jews, he proceeded to seize Peter also. This happened during the Feast of Unleavened Bread. After arresting him, he put him in prison, handing him over to be guarded by four squads of four soldiers each. Herod intended to bring him out for public trial after the Passover.

So Peter was kept in prison, but the church was earnestly praying to God for him.

The night before Herod was to bring him to trial, Peter was sleeping between two soldiers, bound with two chains, and sentries stood guard at the entrance. Suddenly an angel of the Lord appeared and a light shone in the cell. He struck Peter on the side and woke him up. "Quick, get up!" he said, and the chains fell off Peter's wrists.

Then the angel said to him, "Put on your clothes and sandals." And Peter did so. "Wrap your cloak around you and follow me," the angel told him. Peter followed him out of the prison, but he had no idea that what the angel was doing was really happening; he thought he was seeing a vision. They passed the first and second guards and came to the iron gate leading to the city. It opened for them by itself, and they went through it. When they had walked the length of one street, suddenly the angel left him.

Then Peter came to himself and said, "Now I know without a doubt that the Lord sent his angel and rescued me from Herod's clutches and from everything the Jewish people were anticipating."

When this had dawned on him, he went to the house of Mary the mother of John, also called Mark, where many people had gathered and were praying. Peter knocked at the outer entrance, and a servant girl named Rhoda came to answer the door. When she recognized Peter's voice, she was so overjoyed she ran back without opening it and exclaimed, "Peter is at the door!"

"You're out of your mind," they told her. When she kept insisting that it was so, they said, "It must be his angel."

But Peter kept on knocking, and when they opened the door and saw him, they were astonished. Peter motioned with his hand for them to be quiet and described how the Lord had brought him out of prison. "Tell James and the brothers about this," he said, and then he left for another place.

In the morning, there was no small commotion among the soldiers as to what had become of Peter. After Herod had a thorough search made for him and did not find him, he cross-examined the guards and ordered that they be executed. (Acts 12:1-19)

In commenting on this episode, I can do no better than Patrick Henry Reardon, who wrote the following on his "Daily Reflections" website.

For a proper understanding of this story of Peter's imprisonment, it is important to make note of the time when the event happens. Peter is delivered from prison at the Passover, the very night commemorating Israel's deliverance from bondage in Egypt. As the angel of the Lord came through the land that night to remove Israel's chains by slaying the first-born of Israel's oppressors, so the delivering angel returns to strike the fetters from Peter's hands and lead him forth from the dungeon. And as Israel's earlier liberation foreshadowed that Paschal Mystery whereby Jesus our Lord led all of us from our servitude to the satanic Pharaoh by rising from the dead, so we observe aspects of the Resurrection in Peter's deliverance from prison. Like the tomb of Jesus, Peter's cell is guarded by soldiers (verses 4,6). That cell, again like the tomb of Jesus, is invaded by a radiant angelic presence, and the very command to Peter is to "arise" (*anasta* – verse 7). It is no wonder that in regarding Rafael's famous chiaroscuro depiction of this scene in the apartments in the Vatican (over the window in the Stanza of Heliodorus), the viewer must look very closely, for his first impression is that he is looking at a traditional portrayal of the Lord's Resurrection. And what is the Church doing during all that night of the Passover? Praying (verses 5,12); indeed, it is our first record of a Paschal Vigil Service. Peter's guards, alas, must share the fate of Egypt's first-born sons (verse 19).[9]

Stage One Complete

For the Israelites, the journey to the Promised Land began with simply getting out of Egypt. To do that they had to follow Moses as he followed God, who exercised his power and authority over the gods of Egypt and forgave the sins of the people by placing their punishment on the lamb. They had to fall in line behind Moses and under the blood of the lamb in order to have a shot at making it to the Promised Land.

For us, the way out of slavery on this planet is to follow Jesus, who *is* God. Jesus exercised his power and authority over Satan and his demons and then took the punishment for our sins on himself. We have to fall in line behind Jesus and under his blood in order to have our shot at the Promised Land. While we do not physically have to put his blood on the doorposts of our house, by acknowledging our need for a savior and repenting of our rebellion against God, we spiritually place his blood on the doorposts of our heart and walk under the blood of the lamb. Of course, this step is just the beginning. Now the tough part of the journey begins.

PART II

Across the Wilderness

The Nature of the Journey

CHAPTER 4

The Call to Discipleship

So God led the people around by the desert road toward the Red Sea. The Israelites went up out of Egypt armed for battle.

EXODUS 13:18

Anyone who does not carry his cross and follow me cannot be my disciple.

LUKE 14:27

The way some people talk about Christianity, I get the impression that they think this book should have ended already. After all, I have covered Jesus' death and have explained how he is, to use a common theological term, our substitutionary atonement. That is to say, Jesus took the just wrath of God that was to be poured out on us upon himself. He took our place, became our substitute, and received our punishment in order to atone for our sins. Combined with the resurrection, this made it possible for us to be in relationship with God.

For some, there isn't much more to the gospel message. They speak about salvation as a one-time event in which a person intellectually assents to these truths about God's work (and perhaps some other propositions about God and Jesus) and admits that he or she is a sinner. That person then may be encouraged to do other things as part of being a Christian, but generally those things are considered extras. In this understanding of salvation, salvation is accomplished at the time of leaving slavery. As long as one has gone "under the blood," salvation is complete. From that point on, the redemption experience is referred to in past tense. Having punched their ticket, one who has been saved can spend the rest of their life waiting for the day when Jesus will welcome them into Heaven.

Within this framework, Jesus' call is understood as an appeal to make a one-time "decision" for him. The specifics of this salvation experience can vary depending on the theological tradition, but it is likely to include a person repenting of his or her sins and accepting certain propositions about Jesus' divinity and work. It also may involve a vow to try to live a godly life. Practically speaking, though, the moment of decision is understood to be the main thing. After that, the Christian can be content resting in their salvation, essentially killing time until they die or Jesus comes back to get them.

However, if the story of the Exodus is to be our guide (and I think we will continue to see that it should), we cannot take this approach. There is nothing wrong with making a decision for Christ. Indeed, I have encouraged it already in this book as a necessary starting point for the journey. Nevertheless, it is just that – a starting point. It is not the entirety of salvation.[11]

God wanted more than a one-time decision from the Hebrews. He did not treat the act of putting blood over the door as an automatic ticket into the Promised Land. God wanted more than one night of ritualistic obedience. Instead he wanted a lifetime of complete submission to his will. Only this would actually get the Israelites into Canaan.

If the Passover was the end of the story, I think we could have expected to see something along these lines. God should immediately (or at least very quickly) have plopped the Children of Israel down in the Promised Land, as they had accomplished his entrance requirements. At the very least he should have handed out "Get into Canaan Free" cards and told the people to present them at the border when they arrived. Neither of those things happened.

There was no Star Trek-like transporter to beam the Israelites up out of Egypt as soon as they trusted God by placing the blood over their doors. We don't read of them being re-animated instantly inside the Promised Land. God didn't tell them to go and find their own way in life, waiting for the Promised Land to be ready for them.

Instead, God led the Israelites hour by hour. He guided them using a cloud by day and fire by night. Rather than tell the people to go it on their own, he demanded that they fall in line behind him and submit to his direction. He didn't even take them along the shortest route: "When Pharaoh let the people go, God did not lead them on the road through the Philistine country, though that was shorter. For God said, 'If they face war, they might change their minds and return to Egypt.' So God led the people around by the desert road toward the Red Sea. The Israelites went up out of Egypt armed for battle" (Exodus 13:17-18).

"By day the LORD went ahead of them in a pillar of cloud to guide them on their way and by night in a pillar of fire to give them light, so that they could travel by day or night. Neither the pillar of cloud by day nor the pillar of fire by night left its place in front of the people" (Exodus 13:21-22).

Later we read just how closely the Israelites were to rely on God's direction: "In all the travels of the Israelites, whenever the cloud lifted from above the tabernacle, they would set out; but if the cloud did not lift, they did not set out – until the day it lifted" (Exodus 40:36-37).

The Passover and exit from Egypt was not the complete salvation experience. It was just the first step. It was the beginning of a long journey lived in submission to God's plan. The Passover was the beginning of an endurance race and a hard battle. God called the Israelites to follow him – to place their hopes and dreams in his hands and submit their will to his, even to the point of wandering without a permanent home and taking up arms against their enemies. It was a radical call.

The Narrow Road

Jesus presents us with the same radical call. He did not go around offering "Get into Heaven Free" cards. He did not implore his listeners to make a one-time decision that would seal the deal forever. Rather, he called men and women to follow him, to submit their hopes and dreams to him, to become his disciples. The Israelites came out of Egypt armed to fight and ready to walk, because God had called them to a battle and a journey. That is exactly the same call Jesus gives to us. He says, "Enter through the narrow gate. For wide is the gate and broad is the road that leads to destruction, and many enter through it. But small is the gate and narrow the road that leads to life, and only a few find it" (Matthew 7:13-14).

Notice that the gate is just a starting point. It opens to the road, on which we spend our Christian life traveling. Jesus' call is not just to believe that he is God or make a spiritual decision of some kind (although it is certainly includes both), but to give up your will to his and to follow him.

As Jesus was walking beside the Sea of Galilee, he
saw two brothers, Simon called Peter and his brother
Andrew. They were casting a net into the lake, for
they were fishermen. "Come, follow me," Jesus said,
"and I will make you fishers of men." At once they
left their nets and followed him. Going on from there,
he saw two other brothers, James son of Zebedee and
his brother John. They were in a boat with their father
Zebedee, preparing their nets. Jesus called them, and
immediately they left the boat and their father and
followed him. (Matthew 4:18-22)

This narrow road is not an easy path, as Jesus makes clear.
It will involve hardship and deprivation and quite possibly
the loss of many things we hold dear. As we just read, it cost
the first disciples their livelihood and family ties. Of course,
being a journey that is also a battle, this is just what Jesus
said it would cost, at least potentially. He said,

Do not suppose that I have come to bring peace to
the earth. I did not come to bring peace, but a sword.
For I have come to turn 'a man against his father,
a daughter against her mother, a daughter-in-law
against her mother-in-law – a man's enemies will be
the members of his own household.'

Anyone who loves his father or mother more than
me is not worthy of me; anyone who loves his son
or daughter more than me is not worthy of me; and
anyone who does not take his cross and follow me
is not worthy of me. Whoever finds his life will lose
it, and whoever loses his life for my sake will find it.
(Matthew 10:34-39)

By its very nature, the act of joining sides in a war draws distinctions between people, even friends and family. In the same way, setting out on a journey causes separation between even the closest of allies. If you are a soldier or a sojourner, people are either with you or they are not. Jesus' call is to join his revolution and travel the narrow road to Heaven. Anything that attempts to keep you from this task must be left behind. "The man who loves his life will lose it, while the man who hates his life in this world will keep it for eternal life. Whoever serves me must follow me; and where I am, my servant also will be. My Father will honor the one who serves me" (John 12:25-26).

Those that think salvation is a one-time decision often try to make that decision as simple and easy as possible for people when evangelizing. They make no harsh demands and do not talk of a future life of discipleship. They downplay or ignore any parts of Jesus' message that may make a person uncomfortable and instead emphasize the more "positive" aspects of the gospel.

Jesus did exactly the opposite. Because he knew that salvation was not the work of a moment, but rather a lifetime, and that following him meant joining sides in a war and setting off on a difficult journey, Jesus took care to make sure his listeners understood just how much discipleship would cost them. He didn't water down the message to make it more appealing. On the contrary, Jesus emphasized the difficulty of the charge.

> When Jesus saw the crowd around him, he gave orders to cross to the other side of the lake. Then a teacher of the law came to him and said, "Teacher, I will follow you wherever you go."

Jesus replied, "Foxes have holes and birds of the air have nests, but the Son of Man has no place to lay his head."

Another disciple said to him, "Lord, first let me go and bury my father."

But Jesus told him, "Follow me, and let the dead bury their own dead." (Matthew 8:18-22)

The first man seemed eager to follow Jesus. He was what many would consider an ideal candidate for discipleship, a prototypical seeker. Interestingly, Jesus made sure the man understood that if he followed Jesus, he wouldn't have a place to call home. Jesus emphasized the hardship and the long-term discomfort associated with being his disciple.

The second man also seemed interested, but wanted to attend to some family business. In reply, Jesus forbade the man from attending his father's funeral, which seems quite harsh. However, it is unlikely that the man's father was already dead. The man was probably asking to go home and wait for his father to die so that he could get his inheritance and then follow Jesus without having to worry about money. Jesus explained that discipleship does not work that way. You either leave everything and follow or you don't follow at all. Such is the nature of a call to war, or a call to work. Consider this teaching.

Large crowds were traveling with Jesus, and turning to them he said: "If anyone comes to me and does not hate his father and mother, his wife and children, his brothers and sisters – yes, even his own life – he cannot be my disciple. And anyone who does not carry his cross and follow me cannot be my disciple.

"Suppose one of you wants to build a tower. Will he not first sit down and estimate the cost to see if he has enough money to complete it? For if he lays the foundation and is not able to finish it, everyone who sees it will ridicule him, saying, 'This fellow began to build and was not able to finish.'

"Or suppose a king is about to go to war against another king. Will he not first sit down and consider whether he is able with ten thousand men to oppose the one coming against him with twenty thousand? If he is not able, he will send a delegation while the other is still a long way off and will ask for terms of peace. In the same way, any of you who does not give up everything he has cannot be my disciple." (Luke 14:25-35)

The Israelites could have decided that the Promised Land was not worth the effort of crossing the wilderness (and we will see later that many of them ultimately did make this unfortunate choice), but there can be no mistake that this decision is one that leaves them in slavery or death. Deciding to side with the world and take what the world offers is a decision to reject Jesus and reject Heaven. This is what one rich young man did.

Now a man came up to Jesus and asked, "Teacher, what good thing must I do to get eternal life?"

"Why do you ask me about what is good?" Jesus replied. "There is only One who is good. If you want to enter life, obey the commandments."

"Which ones?" the man inquired.

Jesus replied, "'Do not murder, do not commit adultery, do not steal, do not give false testimony, honor your father and mother,' and 'love your neighbor as yourself.'"

"All these I have kept," the young man said. "What do I still lack?"

Jesus answered, "If you want to be perfect, go, sell your possessions and give to the poor, and you will have treasure in heaven. Then come, follow me." When the young man heard this, he went away sad, because he had great wealth.

Then Jesus said to his disciples, "I tell you the truth, it is hard for a rich man to enter the kingdom of heaven. Again I tell you, it is easier for a camel to go through the eye of a needle than for a rich man to enter the kingdom of God."

When the disciples heard this, they were greatly astonished and asked, "Who then can be saved?"

Jesus looked at them and said, "With man this is impossible, but with God all things are possible."

Peter answered him, "We have left everything to follow you! What then will there be for us?"

Jesus said to them, "I tell you the truth, at the renewal of all things, when the Son of Man sits on his glorious throne, you who have followed me will also sit on twelve thrones, judging the twelve tribes of Israel. And everyone who has left houses or brothers or sisters or father or mother or children or fields for my sake will receive a hundred times as much and will inherit eternal life. But many who are first will be last, and many who are last will be first." (Matthew 19:16-30)

As Jesus made clear at the end of that teaching, the benefits of following him are tremendous. It is important to understand, though, that you don't receive all those benefits right away. At first, following Jesus means leaving your comfort zone to set out into the wilderness to fight. Those that are unwilling to do that, like the rich young man, may look like they are first here and now, but ultimately they will end up last. On the other hand, those that give up everything and follow, like the disciples, seem to be last here and now, but will end up first.

What good is avoiding the wilderness now if you end up in Hell for eternity? The wilderness leads to the Promised Land. The narrow road leads to Heaven. The Kingdom of God wins. If you know which path leads to Paradise and which army is going to be victorious in the end, shouldn't you take that path and join that side, no matter how difficult it may make your life in the interim? Jesus made this exact argument:

> Then he called the crowd to him along with his disciples and said: "If anyone would come after me, he must deny himself and take up his cross and follow me. For whoever wants to save his life will lose it, but whoever loses his life for me and for the gospel will save it. What good is it for a man to gain the whole world, yet forfeit his soul? Or what can a man give in exchange for his soul? If anyone is ashamed of me and my words in this adulterous and sinful generation, the Son of Man will be ashamed of him

when he comes in his Father's glory with the holy angels." (Mark 8:34-38)

The call of Jesus, then, is to take up your cross and lose your life. German theologian Dietrich Bonhoeffer wrote, "When God calls a man, he bids him come and die."[12] By this he meant that a man has to give up everything he holds dear and submit his entire self to the will of God. Bonhoeffer was talking about the spiritual, intellectual and emotional dimension of life, to be sure, but he also meant the physical. We are to love God to the point of not shrinking back even from physical death in the course of following God's call.

Bonhoeffer was not mouthing empty platitudes. He understood the call to death in every sense of the word. An outspoken critic of the Nazis during World War II, Bonhoeffer had plenty of opportunity to safely wait out the war working as an academic in America. However, he decided that God wanted him back in Germany, working with the resistance movement to free his homeland. After being arrested for taking part in an unsuccessful attempt on Hitler's life, Bonhoeffer was hanged in Flossenburg concentration camp on April 9, 1945, just three weeks before it was liberated by the Allies.

The Bible agrees that the call of Christ is a call to die, sometimes even physically. Look at the radical commission Jesus gave Peter.

> When they had finished eating, Jesus said to Simon Peter, "Simon son of John, do you truly love me more than these?"
>
> "Yes, Lord," he said, "you know that I love you."
>
> Jesus said, "Feed my lambs."

Again Jesus said, "Simon son of John, do you truly love me?"

He answered, "Yes, Lord, you know that I love you."

Jesus said, "Take care of my sheep."

The third time he said to him, "Simon son of John, do you love me?"

Peter was hurt because Jesus asked him the third time, "Do you love me?" He said, "Lord, you know all things; you know that I love you."

Jesus said, "Feed my sheep. I tell you the truth, when you were younger you dressed yourself and went where you wanted; but when you are old you will stretch out your hands, and someone else will dress you and lead you where you do not want to go." Jesus said this to indicate the kind of death by which Peter would glorify God. Then he said to him, "Follow me!" (John 21:15-19)

Three times Jesus asked Peter if he loved Christ more than anything else in the world, and three times Peter was told to work at his pastoral calling. Then the kicker: Jesus told Peter explicitly that this calling is going to lead directly to Peter's death! The cost of discipleship doesn't get any more expensive than that.

The writer of Hebrews describes the heroes of the faith this way:

Some faced jeers and flogging, while still others were chained and put in prison. They were stoned; they were sawed in two; they were put to death by the sword. They went about in sheepskins and goatskins, destitute, persecuted and mistreated – the world was not worthy of them. They wandered in deserts and mountains, and in caves and holes in the ground. These were all commended for their faith, yet none of them received what had been promised. God had planned something better for us so that only together with us would they be made perfect. (Hebrews 11:36-40)

What should we do to emulate these brave souls? Notice the race terminology in the conclusion of the passage:

Therefore, since we are surrounded by such a great cloud of witnesses, let us throw off everything that hinders and the sin that so easily entangles, and let us run with perseverance the race marked out for us. Let us fix our eyes on Jesus, the author and perfecter of our faith, who for the joy set before him endured the cross, scorning its shame, and sat down at the right hand of the throne of God. Consider him who endured such opposition from sinful men, so that you will not grow weary and lose heart. In your struggle against sin, you have not yet resisted to the point of shedding your blood. (Hebrews 12:1-4)

Isn't that amazing? One of the points of this passage is that those who are struggling along the narrow road should take heart because, after all, they haven't had to follow the great heroes of the faith and die! At least not yet! They "have not yet resisted to the point" of death. The implication is clear – they might have to do just that.

Of course, as we also see in this passage, the greatest example of self-denial and radical faith was Jesus himself.

His submission to the will of the Father was absolute. When faced with nothing less than excruciating torture and death on a cross, Jesus submitted to the will of the Father in the Garden of Gethsemane.

> Then Jesus went with his disciples to a place called Gethsemane, and he said to them, "Sit here while I go over there and pray." He took Peter and the two sons of Zebedee along with him, and he began to be sorrowful and troubled. Then he said to them, "My soul is overwhelmed with sorrow to the point of death. Stay here and keep watch with me."
>
> Going a little farther, he fell with his face to the ground and prayed, "My Father, if it is possible, may this cup be taken from me. Yet not as I will, but as you will."
>
> Then he returned to his disciples and found them sleeping. "Could you men not keep watch with me for one hour?" he asked Peter. "Watch and pray so that you will not fall into temptation. The spirit is willing, but the body is weak."
>
> He went away a second time and prayed, "My Father, if it is not possible for this cup to be taken away unless I drink it, may your will be done."
>
> When he came back, he again found them sleeping, because their eyes were heavy. So he left them and went away once more and prayed the third time, saying the same thing. (Matthew 26:36-44)

This is to be our approach to discipleship as well. Our prayer should be "Not my will but yours be done, Father, even if it means death."

Your attitude should be the same as that of Christ
Jesus: Who, being in very nature God, did not consider
equality with God something to be grasped, but made
himself nothing, taking the very nature of a servant,
being made in human likeness. And being found in
appearance as a man, he humbled himself and became
obedient to death—even death on a cross! (Philippians
2:5-8)

*Other New Testament References to the Christian Life as a
Journey and Battle*

The portrait of the Christian life as a journey (or a race)
and a battle is painted often in scripture. Followers of Jesus
are continually referred to as soldiers and athletes. For
example, the church in Corinth is encouraged with these
words:

Do you not know that in a race all the runners run,
but only one gets the prize? Run in such a way as to
get the prize. Everyone who competes in the games
goes into strict training. They do it to get a crown that
will not last; but we do it to get a crown that will last
forever. Therefore I do not run like a man running
aimlessly; I do not fight like a man beating the air.
No, I beat my body and make it my slave so that
after I have preached to others, I myself will not be
disqualified for the prize. (1 Corinthians 9:24-27)

Paul questions the Galatians using similar language:
"You were running a good race. Who cut in on you and kept
you from obeying the truth?" (Galatians 5:7). On a more
military note, the Ephesians are told:

Put on the full armor of God so that you can take your stand against the devil's schemes. For our struggle is not against flesh and blood, but against the rulers, against the authorities, against the powers of this dark world and against the spiritual forces of evil in the heavenly realms. Therefore put on the full armor of God, so that when the day of evil comes, you may be able to stand your ground, and after you have done everything, to stand. Stand firm then, with the belt of truth buckled around your waist, with the breastplate of righteousness in place, and with your feet fitted with the readiness that comes from the gospel of peace. In addition to all this, take up the shield of faith, with which you can extinguish all the flaming arrows of the evil one. Take the helmet of salvation and the sword of the Spirit, which is the word of God. And pray in the Spirit on all occasions with all kinds of prayers and requests. With this in mind, be alert and always keep on praying for all the saints. (Ephesians 6:11-18)

As is clear from that passage, "Though we live in the world, we do not wage war as the world does. The weapons we fight with are not the weapons of the world. On the contrary, they have divine power to demolish strongholds" (2 Corinthians 10:3-4). Peter warns: "Be self-controlled and alert. Your enemy the devil prowls around like a roaring lion looking for someone to devour. Resist him, standing firm in the faith, because you know that your brothers throughout the world are undergoing the same kind of sufferings" (1 Peter 5:8-9).

With that in mind, young pastor Timothy is told: "Fight the good fight of the faith. Take hold of the eternal life to which you were called when you made your good confession in the presence of many witnesses" (1 Timothy 6:12).

In the second letter to Timothy, Paul explains further that his apprentice should, "Endure hardship with us like a good soldier of Christ Jesus. No one serving as a soldier gets involved in civilian affairs – he wants to please his commanding officer. Similarly, if anyone competes as an athlete, he does not receive the victor's crown unless he competes according to the rules" (2 Timothy 2:3-5).

The fact that the Christian life is a race and a battle is clear. Salvation is not a one-time act, nor is it a free pass to do whatever you want with your life until Jesus takes you to Heaven. It is a radical call to give up everything and follow Jesus, joining his army as travels and fights its way across the wilderness to the Promised Land.

At the very end of his life, Paul, who constantly referred to himself as a "slave of Christ" (Romans 1:1, Philippians 1:1 and Titus 1:1, for example), looks ahead to finally arriving in Heaven. He doesn't say, "I'm glad I've got my entry card" or "I hope Jesus remembers me from that one time that we met." Instead he says, "I have fought the good fight, I have finished the race, I have kept the faith" (2 Timothy 4:7). May that be our testimony as well.

CHAPTER 5

God's Reason for Everything

I will gain glory through Pharaoh and all his
army, through his chariots and his horsemen. The
Egyptians will know that I am the LORD when I
gain glory through Pharaoh, his chariots and his
horsemen.

EXODUS 14:17-18

Then I heard what sounded like a great multitude,
like the roar of rushing waters and like loud peals
of thunder, shouting: "Hallelujah! For our Lord
God Almighty reigns. Let us rejoice and be glad
and give him glory!"

REVELATION 19:6-7a

God's Delight in Being God[13]

Before venturing too far into the wilderness adventures of
the Israelites, I want to use this chapter to address God's
motivation and answer the question "Why is God doing all

this? Why does God go to all the trouble of redeeming people from captivity?"

This may seem like a no-brainer. Because he loved the Israelites and he loves us, right? He saved the Israelites because they were special, and he saves us because we are special. In fact, I often hear that God's overwhelming love and esteem for us is his motivation for everything. A book my young daughters recently received as a gift teaches that God created the world and made humans so that he could love them. I'm sorry to burst anyone's bubble, but this is simply not the case.

It's not that God doesn't love us, and I am not saying that he didn't have people in mind when he created the universe or set out to redeem mankind. However, he was not acting primarily out of his love for us. While God certainly loves each of us, this unhealthy focus on our supposed crucial part in the big scheme of things makes us the center of the universe instead of God. We talk as if God acts to glorify us. He doesn't. God acts to glorify himself. Everything he does flows from this motivation.

The word glory literally means weight. It refers to the substance of something. When speaking of God's glory, the term often refers to God's substantive excellence, his greatness of being. It also sometimes means the external manifestation of this excellence as well as the celebration of that excellence by others. So when I say that God's glory is the reason for everything he does, I am saying that everything God does is an external manifestation of His inner excellence and is designed to be recognized and celebrated as such. All of God's actions spring out of His delight in being God and his desire for others to delight in him being God. The first evidence for this claim is found in creation.

The Glory of God in Creation

When God created the world and us, he was acting out of this passion for his own glory. God did not need to create the universe or us. He was not lonely or incomplete, as this would make him less than God. He was and is completely satisfied and content; indeed he delights and has always delighted in simply being God. Creation resulted from a bubbling over of this delight. God's joy overflowed like a fountain in creation and everything that resulted is intended to glorify him. "The heavens declare the glory of God; the skies proclaim the work of his hands" (Psalm 19:1). Why do they do this? Because that is what they were created to do. God's glory is revealed through his creation. Paul explains in Romans "For since the creation of the world God's invisible qualities – his eternal power and divine nature – have been clearly seen, being understood from what has been made" (Romans 1:20). God's intention in creating the universe was to show his greatness.

Man is the most explicit demonstration of that greatness. The creation account in Genesis reaches its high point with Adam and Eve.

> Then God said, "Let us make man in our image, in our likeness, and let them rule over the fish of the sea and the birds of the air, over the livestock, over all the earth, and over all the creatures that move along the ground." So God created man in his own image, in the image of God he created him; male and female he created them. (Genesis 1:26)

God's greatest creation was humans, because they are made in the very image of God and therefore glorify him the most. "Bring my sons from afar and my daughters from the ends of the earth – everyone who is called by my name, whom I created for my glory, whom I formed and made" (Isaiah 43:6b-7). "The wild animals honor me, the jackals and the owls, because I provide water in the desert and streams in the wasteland, to give drink to my people, my chosen, the people I formed for myself that they may proclaim my praise" (Isaiah 43:20-21).

The Glory of God in Redeeming Israel

God's passion for his glory motivates not only his creative endeavors, but everything he does. In the rest of the chapter we will look at some scriptural evidence to support this claim and see how God's passion for his glory motivated his redemptive work on behalf of the Israelites as well as the redemptive work he has done (and is doing) for us. We will see that God released the Israelites from bondage and remained faithful to them through the wilderness because of his passion for his glory. We will then see how God frees and remains faithful to us for the very same reason.

As I mentioned last chapter, God did not lead the Israelites by the shortest route to the Promised Land. Instead he turned them toward the Red Sea (Exodus 13:18). Then God made a strange request of Moses, at least from a strategic military standpoint. He told them to make camp backed up against the sea: "Then the LORD said to Moses, 'Tell the Israelites to turn back and encamp near Pi Hahiroth, between Migdol and the sea. They are to encamp by the sea, directly opposite Baal Zephon'" (Exodus 14:1-2).

Why would God do this? Didn't he know that the Israelites would be vulnerable to attack? Yes, and that is why he did it. God intended to bring glory to himself through one more tremendous miracle. He explained to Moses, "Pharaoh will think, 'The Israelites are wandering around the land in confusion, hemmed in by the desert.' And I will harden Pharaoh's heart, and he will pursue them. But I will gain glory for myself through Pharaoh and all his army, and the Egyptians will know that I am the LORD" (Exodus 14:3-4).

The Israelites obeyed and you probably know what happened next. Pharaoh did bring his armies after the Israelites and had them pinned down against the Red Sea. All looked lost and they cried out to God for help.

> Then the LORD said to Moses, "Why are you crying out to me? Tell the Israelites to move on. Raise your staff and stretch out your hand over the sea to divide the water so that the Israelites can go through the sea on dry ground. I will harden the hearts of the Egyptians so that they will go in after them. And I will gain glory through Pharaoh and all his army, through his chariots and his horsemen. The Egyptians will know that I am the LORD when I gain glory through Pharaoh, his chariots and his horsemen."

> Then the angel of God, who had been traveling in front of Israel's army, withdrew and went behind them. The pillar of cloud also moved from in front and stood behind them, coming between the armies of Egypt and Israel. Throughout the night the cloud brought darkness to the one side and light to the other side; so neither went near the other all night long.

> Then Moses stretched out his hand over the sea, and all that night the LORD drove the sea back with a strong east wind and turned it into dry land. The waters were divided, and the Israelites went through the sea on dry ground, with a wall of water on their right and on their left.

> The Egyptians pursued them, and all Pharaoh's horses and chariots and horsemen followed them into

the sea. During the last watch of the night the LORD looked down from the pillar of fire and cloud at the Egyptian army and threw it into confusion. He made the wheels of their chariots come off so that they had difficulty driving. And the Egyptians said, "Let's get away from the Israelites! The LORD is fighting for them against Egypt."

Then the LORD said to Moses, "Stretch out your hand over the sea so that the waters may flow back over the Egyptians and their chariots and horsemen." Moses stretched out his hand over the sea, and at daybreak the sea went back to its place. The Egyptians were fleeing toward it, and the LORD swept them into the sea. The water flowed back and covered the chariots and horsemen – the entire army of Pharaoh that had followed the Israelites into the sea. Not one of them survived.

But the Israelites went through the sea on dry ground, with a wall of water on their right and on their left. That day the LORD saved Israel from the hands of the Egyptians, and Israel saw the Egyptians lying dead on the shore. And when the Israelites saw the great power the LORD displayed against the Egyptians, the people feared the LORD and put their trust in him and in Moses his servant. (Exodus 14:15-31)

Mission accomplished. God was glorified and the people trusted in him. Another way of putting this is to say that God's name was exalted. God's reputation was upheld. The truth about his greatness was made known and praised through a display of his power and his redemption of the Israelites. This is just what God had previously explained to Pharaoh would happen: "For by now I could have stretched out my hand and struck you and your people with a plague that would have wiped you off the earth. But I have raised you up for this very purpose, that I might show you my power and that my name might be proclaimed in all the earth" (Exodus 9:15-16).

In future years the Israelites would look back at the Exodus and recall what had happened and why. Isaiah wrote that "his people remembered the days of old" and asked,

> Where is he...who sent his glorious arm of power to be at Moses' right hand, who divided the waters before them, to gain for himself everlasting renown, who led them through the depths? Like a horse in open country, they did not stumble; like cattle that go down to the plain, they were given rest by the Spirit of the Lord. This is how you guided your people to make for yourself a glorious name. (Isaiah 63:12-14)

When David was called to build a temple for God, he responded with appropriate understanding of God's motivation.

> How great you are, O Sovereign LORD! There is no one like you, and there is no God but you, as we have heard with our own ears. And who is like your people Israel – the one nation on earth that God went out to redeem as a people for himself, and to make a name for himself, and to perform great and awesome wonders by driving out nations and their gods from before your people, whom you redeemed from Egypt? You have established your people Israel as your very own forever, and you, O LORD, have become their God.
>
> And now, LORD God, keep forever the promise you have made concerning your servant and his house. Do as you promised, so that your name will be great

forever. Then men will say, "The LORD Almighty is God over Israel!" (2 Samuel 7:22-26)

The Glory of God in Remaining Faithful to Israel

As we will see as we continue to walk through Exodus, the Israelites didn't always do a very good job of trusting God or remaining faithful to him. However, God always remained faithful to them. He never reneged on his promise. Again, the reason for this was not their innate value or because of his great love, but rather because of God's passion for his glory. The clearest explanation of this is found in Ezekiel. God declares that, although his people have disobeyed, he will still gather them from exile. However, they are not to think that this decision is based on something they did or on some value they possess. It is not for the people's sake that God is acting, but for the sake of his name.

> And wherever they went among the nations they profaned my holy name, for it was said of them, "These are the LORD's people, and yet they had to leave his land." I had concern for my holy name, which the house of Israel profaned among the nations where they had gone.

> Therefore say to the house of Israel, "This is what the Sovereign LORD says: It is not for your sake, O house of Israel, that I am going to do these things, but for the sake of my holy name, which you have profaned among the nations where you have gone. I will show the holiness of my great name, which has been profaned among the nations, the name you have profaned among them. Then the nations will know that I am the LORD, declares the Sovereign LORD, when I show myself holy through you before their eyes.

"For I will take you out of the nations; I will gather you from all the countries and bring you back into your own land. ... I want you to know that I am not doing this for your sake, declares the Sovereign LORD. Be ashamed and disgraced for your conduct, O house of Israel!" (Ezekiel 36:20-24, 32)

In another example, Israel asked for a king so that they could be like the other nations (1 Samuel 8). Samuel proclaimed to them that this was a rejection of God and that they had done an evil thing by asking for a king. When the people pleaded for mercy, Samuel explained why God would not reject them: "For the sake of his great name the LORD will not reject his people, because the LORD was pleased to make you his own" (1 Samuel 12:22).

Joshua had a similarly clear understanding of God's motives. When Israel found itself in trouble, Joshua pleaded with the Lord to save his people. Notice that he argued based on God's passion for his own glory rather than his love for the people or their intrinsic value. "O Lord, what can I say, now that Israel has been routed by its enemies? The Canaanites and the other people of the country will hear about this and they will surround us and wipe out our name from the earth. What then will you do for your own great name?" (Joshua 7:8-9).

God sums up the motivation for his faithfulness and mercy nicely in Isaiah 48: "For my own name's sake I delay my wrath; for the sake of my praise I hold it back from you, so as not to cut you off. See, I have refined you, though not as silver; I have tested you in the furnace of affliction. For my own sake, for my own sake, I do this. How can I let myself be defamed? I will not yield my glory to another" (Isaiah 48:9-11).

The Glory of God in Redeeming and Remaining Faithful to Us

Just as God's passion for his glory is what motivated him to redeem the Israelites, it also motivates him to redeem us. God is not ultimately driven to rescue us by our goodness or value or anything about us at all. Rather, God saves us because he is glorified in saving us. We are not the deciding factor, he is. As Paul explains, in comparing God's salvation of the Israelites to his salvation of us, "It does not, therefore, depend on man's desire or effort, but on God's mercy. For the Scripture says to Pharaoh: 'I raised you up for this very purpose, that I might display my power in you and that my name might be proclaimed in all the earth'" (Romans 9:16-17).

The Psalmist asked God to forgive his sins "For your name's sake" (Psalm 25:11, 79:9) and according to John, God does just that: "I write to you, dear children, because your sins have been forgiven on account of his name" (1 John 2:12).

Not only does God forgive our sins, he also faithfully guides and directs us. "The Lord is my shepherd, I shall not want. He makes me lie down in green pastures; He leads me beside quiet waters. He restores my soul; He guides me in the paths of righteousness for His name's sake" (Psalm 23: 1-3).

Paul explains that this direction includes a call to service on behalf of God's glory. "Through him and for his name's sake, we received grace and apostleship to call people from among all the Gentiles to the obedience that comes from faith" (Romans 1:5).

The same Apostle sums up the motivation for God's redemptive action at the beginning of his letter to the Ephesians. Notice the emphasis on God's glory.

> Praise be to the God and Father of our Lord Jesus Christ, who has blessed us in the heavenly realms with

every spiritual blessing in Christ. For he chose us in him before the creation of the world to be holy and blameless in his sight. In love he predestined us to be adopted as his sons through Jesus Christ, in accordance with his pleasure and will – to the praise of his glorious grace, which he has freely given us in the One he loves. In him we have redemption through his blood, the forgiveness of sins, in accordance with the riches of God's grace that he lavished on us with all wisdom and understanding. And he made known to us the mystery of his will according to his good pleasure, which he purposed in Christ, to be put into effect when the times will have reached their fulfillment – to bring all things in heaven and on earth together under one head, even Christ.

In him we were also chosen, having been predestined according to the plan of him who works out everything in conformity with the purpose of his will, in order that we, who were the first to hope in Christ, might be for the praise of his glory. And you also were included in Christ when you heard the word of truth, the gospel of your salvation. Having believed, you were marked in him with a seal, the promised Holy Spirit, who is a deposit guaranteeing our inheritance until the redemption of those who are God's possession – to the praise of his glory. (Ephesians 1:3-14)

God's glory is the ultimate purpose of salvation. The picture of the future found in Revelation backs up this claim, as the vision of Heaven given to John is full of people glorifying God.

[They] sang the song of Moses the servant of God and the song of the Lamb: "Great and marvelous are your deeds, Lord God Almighty. Just and true are your ways, King of the ages. Who will not fear you, O Lord, and bring glory to your name? For you alone are holy. All nations will come and worship before you, for your righteous acts have been revealed." (Revelation 15:3-4)

After this I heard what sounded like the roar of a great multitude in heaven shouting: "Hallelujah! Salvation and glory and power belong to our God, for true and just are his judgments. He has condemned the great prostitute who corrupted the earth by her adulteries. He has avenged on her the blood of his servants." And again they shouted: "Hallelujah! The smoke from her goes up for ever and ever." The twenty-four elders and the four living creatures fell down and worshiped God, who was seated on the throne. And they cried: "Amen, Hallelujah!" Then a voice came from the throne, saying: "Praise our God, all you his servants, you who fear him, both small and great!" Then I heard what sounded like a great multitude, like the roar of rushing waters and like loud peals of thunder, shouting: "Hallelujah! For our Lord God Almighty reigns. Let us rejoice and be glad and give him glory! For the wedding of the Lamb has come, and his bride has made herself ready." (Revelation 19:1-7)

Is God an Egomaniac?

It may seem to you by now that God is a giant egomaniac. When presented with this argument, some people have told me that I make it sound like God is overcome by pride and just needs to get over himself. Is this the case? Of course not. The reason this cannot be so is that God could never put undo focus on himself. On the other hand, we can certainly put undo focus on ourselves. God is worthy of all the focus and praise he can get; we are not.

The reason pride is wrong for us is that we are not deserving to receive glory. Pride used to be referred to as "vain-glory," and I think that term does an excellent job of describing the problem. Pride is glory that is given in vain. It is glory that should not be given because the object of the glory is not glorious. We should not focus on and praise ourselves because we are not worthy to be focused on and praised. However, God is. He is worthy of all glory and honor and therefore can never be guilty of vain-glory.

God is the only independent one. Everything else and everyone else is dependent on him. It is fine for God to consider himself the center of all because he *is* the center of all. It is fine for God to accept worship (worship means to have worth ascribed) because he is worthy. God is above all. He is the most valuable entity there is. It is not alright for me to accept that same worship because I am not. For me to ascribe worth to something that is not worthy is foolishness.

For example, we ascribe different amounts of worth to different things. Gold has a certain amount of value, and silver has another. We generally agree that gold is more valuable than silver, and we would think it foolish for someone to worship silver to such an extent that he would trade two ounces of gold for an ounce of silver. To do so would be to practice vain-glory. Now you might say that precious metals are valued somewhat subjectively, and you wouldn't judge too harshly if someone happened to like silver better than gold. Fair enough. But what about this situation? Suppose a person valued silver more than his relationship to his wife? Or the life of his child? What if a man was willing to trade his son or daughter into slavery for a few ounces of metal? I hope that we find this situation easier to judge, as it is very objective. This would simply be wrong. The life of a child and one's relationship with a spouse is much more valuable than any amount of money. To worship money over family is to reverse the established order of the universe and should be condemned.

This is why God is so adamant that he will not give his glory to another. To do so is to reverse the order of the universe, and not even God can do that. For God to not take the glory for himself or to delight fully in anything or anyone but himself would be idolatry in the very same way as to ascribe worth to money over people.

When God works for his own glory, when he asks for worship and forbids the worship of anything else, he is simply keeping the universe in proper order. The base sin of mankind is to reject this order. We worship the created thing rather than the creator and bring on ourselves all sorts of trouble.

> The wrath of God is being revealed from heaven against all the godlessness and wickedness of men who suppress the truth by their wickedness, since what may be known about God is plain to them, because God has made it plain to them. For since the creation of the world God's invisible qualities—his eternal power and divine nature—have been clearly seen, being understood from what has been made, so that men are without excuse.

> For although they knew God, they neither glorified him as God nor gave thanks to him, but their thinking became futile and their foolish hearts were darkened. Although they claimed to be wise, they became fools and exchanged the glory of the immortal God for images made to look like mortal man and birds and animals and reptiles.

> Therefore God gave them over in the sinful desires of their hearts to sexual impurity for the degrading

of their bodies with one another. They exchanged the truth of God for a lie, and worshiped and served created things rather than the Creator – who is forever praised. Amen. (Romans 1:18-25)

What About John 3:16?

By now you might be thinking, "But doesn't God love me? Didn't he send Jesus because he loves me? What about John 3:16: 'For God so loved the world that he gave his one and only Son, that whoever believes in him shall not perish but have eternal life?'"

Yes, God loves you, but let's make sure we define love properly and bring that definition to our interpretation of John 3:16. Our culture tends to define love in very unbiblical ways, and we need to be sure to not allow the cultural understanding of love to skew our understanding of God and his Word.

In our culture, the concept of love centers on emotions and subjective value judgments. It is generally understood that to love someone is to highly esteem that person and have nice feelings about them. To say, "I love you" is usually to mean, "I think you are special and thinking about you generates pleasurable feelings inside of me." However, in the Bible, love does not refer primarily to an emotional state. Nor does love necessarily connote anything about another person's value. To love biblically is to act in a self-sacrificing way for the good of others.

Jesus' most famous teaching on love took place on Maundy Thursday: the day before Christ's crucifixion. "Maundy" comes from the Latin *mandatum*, meaning command. It refers to the new commandment Jesus gave to his disciples that day. After washing his disciples' feet and explaining that he was going to be betrayed and would have to leave them, he said, "A new command I give you: Love one another. As I have loved you, so you must love one another. By this all men will know that you are my disciples, if you love one another" (John 13:34-35).

The command to love one another was certainly not new to Jesus' Jewish listeners. They already knew that they were to "love your neighbors as yourself" (Leviticus 19:18). What made this pronouncement new? It was the fact that Jesus said they should love each other *in the same way that Jesus loved them.* That is to say, self-sacrificially.

The broader context of this passage in John is one in which Jesus, the Creator and King of the Universe, not only stooped to wash his disciples' feet, but then gave up his very life that they might be saved from slavery to sin and Satan. They were instructed to act in this same self-sacrificing way toward others. When Jesus repeated the commandment later, he made this plain. "My command is this: Love each other as I have loved you. Greater love has no one than this, that he lay down his life for his friends" (John 15:12-13). John obviously looks back at this teaching as he explains the meaning of love in the first of his epistles.

> This is the message you heard from the beginning: We should love one another. ... This is how we know what love is: Jesus Christ laid down his life for us. And we ought to lay down our lives for our brothers. If anyone has material possessions and sees his brother in need but has no pity on him, how can the love of God be in him? Dear children, let us not love with words or tongue but with actions and in truth. (1 John 3:11, 16-18)

Love is more than nice words and pleasant feelings. It is sacrificial action. When the Bible talks about God loving us, it is primarily speaking of the fact that he acts in a self-sacrificing way for our benefit. John 3:16 is no exception.

When John says, "God so loved the world that he gave his one and only Son," we shouldn't read it, "God thought that we were so valuable and special and felt such overwhelming feelings of affection for us that he wanted to do more than just send flowers, so he sent his only son." Rather, it should read "God loved the world in this extraordinary way: he sent his son to die for us." The act of sending his son to die is an example of God's self-sacrificial action for our good. It is not an expression of his emotions or of our value. John is saying, "Look at the extent to which God will sacrifice (love)! How amazing!" John is not saying, "Look at how much affection he has for us" or "Look at how valuable we are in God's eyes." When Paul writes, "God demonstrates his own love for us in this: While we were still sinners, Christ died for us" (Romans 5:8), he is saying that God demonstrated to what lengths he would go in sacrificial action. He is not saying that God demonstrated how much he thought of us or how emotional he gets over us.

Does God think we are valuable? Of course. But don't let our culture's cheap romanticism and cult of self-esteem mislead you as to what that means. God did not wander though Wal-Mart one day, happen to see you down the aisle, and suddenly realize he had found the most ravishing and valuable creature in the universe. He made you. You have value according to the worth he gave you at creation. This happens to be very, very high, since humans are made in his image (Genesis 1:27), but your value is especially high because you can glorify him more than, say, sheep and birds (Matthew 6:26, 10:31, 12:12).

According to John Piper,

> The love of God for sinners is not his making much of them, but his graciously freeing and empowering them to enjoy making much of him.

As [Jonathan] Edwards says, "God is their good." Therefore, if God would do us good, he must direct us to his worth, not ours. The truth that God's glory and our joy in God are one radically undermines modern views of self-centered love. God-centered grace nullifies the gospel of self-esteem. Today, people typically feel loved if you make much of them and help them feel valued. The bottom line in their happiness is that they are made much of.

Edwards observes, with stunning modern relevance, "True saints have their minds, in the first place, inexpressibly pleased and delighted with ... the things of God. But the dependence of the affections of hypocrites is in a contrary order: they first rejoice ... that they are made so much of by God; and then on that ground, he seems in a sort, lovely to them."[14] In other words, in his view, the bottom line of happiness is that we are granted to see the infinite beauty of God and make much of him forever. Human beings do, in fact, have more value than the birds (Matthew 6:26). But that is not the bottom line of our happiness. It simply means that we were created to magnify God's glory by enjoying him in a way birds never can.[15]

As Piper points out, the fact that God's love for us is not primarily about our value should keep us from loving immaturely. By that I mean that we should not love God only because he values us or even because he does nice things for us. We should love him because of who he is.

My wife Kendra and I have two young daughters. Our major challenge as parents (as all parents can testify) is to try to make our children understand that they are not the center of the universe and that their parents do not exist to grant their every desire. To not attempt this would be to spoil our children and hinder our relationship with them.

For example, if I were to ask my youngest to describe why she likes her daddy, I am quite sure her answer would center on all the things that I do for her. "My daddy plays with me, feeds me, reads books to me, changes me and gets me dressed," etc. Hopefully this will change over time, and as she gets older my daughter will be able to answer somewhat more objectively; "My daddy plays with me and reads to me and he tells people about Jesus and writes neat books," etc.

We need the same maturation in our relationship with God. We need to develop a love for him that is based on more than the fact that "He thinks I am special." It's like those early grade school romances. You don't know a certain person exists until one day you find out that they like you. All of a sudden your opinion of them goes way up. As you hopefully know by now, that is no way to pursue a relationship. If you don't like someone for who they are, rather than what they think of you, you're in trouble.

God's Glory and Our Good

One final note for this chapter: God's glory and your good are not in conflict. It is not detrimental to you to live for God's glory or for God to pursue his glory in your life. If glorifying God is what you were made for, you will only be truly happy when you are doing just that. That is your good. Although God does all that he does for his name's sake, this also means that it is for your sake. God knows you will only be happy glorifying him and that is what he pursues.

We see an example of this in Isaiah 43. Earlier we noted that God explicitly states in verses 7, 21 and 25 that he is acting for his name's sake in saving the Israelites. But in verse 14 he says he is acting for the sake of the Israelites. "This is what the LORD says – your Redeemer, the Holy

One of Israel: 'For your sake I will send to Babylon and bring down as fugitives all the Babylonians, in the ships in which they took pride'" (Isaiah 43:14). This is not contradictory, as this is not an either/or proposition. When God acts for his own sake, he is also acting for ours.

Our Delight in God Being God

So what are we to do with all this information about God's glory? The first thing I would suggest is that we get over ourselves. As Paul said on Mars' Hill in Athens, God doesn't need us, we need him. "The God who made the world and everything in it is the Lord of heaven and earth and does not live in temples built by hands. And he is not served by human hands, as if he needed anything, because he himself gives all men life and breath and everything else" (Acts 17:24-25). Our attitude should be that of the Psalmist: "Not to us, O LORD, not to us but to your name be the glory, because of your love and faithfulness. Why do the nations say, 'Where is their God?' Our God is in heaven; he does whatever pleases him" (Psalm 115:1-3).

Secondly, we should celebrate God's extravagant grace. Even though we do not deserve his sacrificial action, he offers it anyway. God works to save us, not because of who we are or anything we have done, but simply out of his goodness and grace. He is glorified in his action, and he is glorified even more when we praise him for it. After the Children of Israel were delivered through the Red Sea, Moses and Miriam glorified God in this beautiful song.

> I will sing to the LORD, for he is highly exalted. The horse and its rider he has hurled into the sea. The LORD is my strength and my song; he has become my salvation. He is my God, and I will praise him, my father's God, and I will exalt him. The LORD is

a warrior; the LORD is his name. Pharaoh's chariots and his army he has hurled into the sea. The best of Pharaoh's officers are drowned in the Red Sea. The deep waters have covered them; they sank to the depths like a stone.

Your right hand, O LORD, was majestic in power. Your right hand, O LORD, shattered the enemy. In the greatness of your majesty you threw down those who opposed you. You unleashed your burning anger; it consumed them like stubble. By the blast of your nostrils the waters piled up. The surging waters stood firm like a wall; the deep waters congealed in the heart of the sea.

The enemy boasted, 'I will pursue, I will overtake them. I will divide the spoils; I will gorge myself on them. I will draw my sword and my hand will destroy them.' But you blew with your breath, and the sea covered them. They sank like lead in the mighty waters.

Who among the gods is like you, O LORD? Who is like you – majestic in holiness, awesome in glory, working wonders? You stretched out your right hand and the earth swallowed them.

In your unfailing love you will lead the people you have redeemed. In your strength you will guide them to your holy dwelling. The nations will hear and tremble; anguish will grip the people of Philistia. The chiefs of Edom will be terrified, the leaders of Moab will be seized with trembling, the people of Canaan will melt away; terror and dread will fall upon them. By the power of your arm they will be as still as a stone – until your people pass by, O LORD, until the people you bought pass by. You will bring them in and plant them on the mountain of your inheritance – the place, O LORD, you made for your dwelling, the sanctuary, O Lord, your hands established. The LORD will reign for ever and ever. (Exodus 15:1-18)

The biblical account of the Red Sea celebration concludes with a summary: "Miriam sang to them: 'Sing to the LORD, for he is highly exalted. The horse and its rider he has hurled into the sea.'" (Exodus 15:21).

Perhaps David was thinking of this episode when he later wrote "You who fear the LORD, praise him! All you descendants of Jacob, honor him! Revere him, all you descendants of Israel!" (Psalm 22:23).

Jonathan Edwards notes, "The end of the creation is that the creation might glorify [God]. Now what is glorifying God, but a rejoicing in that glory he has displayed. The happiness of the creature consists in rejoicing in God, by which also God is magnified and exalted."[16]

We will cover some other ways to glorify God more completely in later chapters. These include doing good works (Matthew 5:16) and bearing fruit (John 15:8). The bottom line is that we should acknowledge and celebrate God's excellence in everything.

> Each one should use whatever gift he has received to serve others, faithfully administering God's grace in its various forms. If anyone speaks, he should do it as one speaking the very words of God. If anyone serves, he should do it with the strength God provides, so that in all things God may be praised through Jesus Christ. To him be the glory and the power for ever and ever. Amen. (1 Peter 4:10-11)

"So whether you eat or drink or whatever you do, do it all for the glory of God" (1 Corinthians 10:31). Just as his glory is the reason for everything God does, so his glory should be the reason for everything we do.

CHAPTER 6

Faith

Remember how the LORD your God led you all the way in the desert these forty years, to humble you and to test you in order to know what was in your heart, whether or not you would keep his commands. He humbled you, causing you to hunger and then feeding you with manna, which neither you nor your fathers had known, to teach you that man does not live on bread alone but on every word that comes from the mouth of the LORD.

DEUTERONOMY 8:2-3

For it is by grace you have been saved, through faith – and this not from yourselves, it is the gift of God – not by works, so that no one can boast.

EPHESIANS 2:8

As we have seen, the plan of salvation, both for the Israelites and for us, is very God-focused. It simply does not happen apart from him. The Israelites were helpless to save themselves and so are we. God takes the initiative in salvation and provides the means to see it accomplished. We contribute no power or wisdom to the process. Nor do we provide the motivation. As we read last chapter, God does it all for his glory. We don't deserve salvation and can do nothing to earn it or convince God to make it happen. It is all his grace.

Having established that, I want to take some time to discuss the fact that humans are not completely passive in salvation. We do have a part to play. That part is to respond to God's grace with faith. When God pours out his unmerited blessing on us, our responsibility is to trust him and obey. Faith is the one thing required of humans for salvation. As the popular scripture attests, we are saved by God's grace, through faith (Ephesians 2:8). But what does that mean, really? What is faith? Why is it required by God? How do we know if we have it? And what is the relationship between faith and works? We will address those questions in the next two chapters.

What Is Faith?

Faith, according to the Bible, "is being sure of what we hope for and certain of what we do not see" (Hebrews 11:1). It is a belief, usually about some event in the future. To have faith is to trust that something will come to pass. It is also to trust that something or someone will be able to bring that event about. Faith always has an object. The object of our faith is whatever or whoever we think will be able to bring about a particular event.

For example, many people have faith that their latter years will be comfortable and free of hard work. They trust that they will be able to retire into a life of relative ease and are therefore confident about the future. Inevitably, that confidence is based on something. It might be a large bank account or stock portfolio, personal talent and charisma, friends in high places, or perhaps a job they are sure will not be lost. These are objects of faith. In the same way, people who are not so sure about the future may be anxious because they lack these things. These people are still placing their faith in money and talent, etc., but because they don't have them, they are not confident about the future.

It is important to know what we are placing our faith in because the road to the Promised Land is passable only by placing our faith in God. He has to be the sole object of our trust. This is what the Bible means when it says we are saved by faith. Saving faith is trust that is placed in God alone. In order to get the freedom they desired, the Israelites had to trust that the God of Moses could deliver on his promises. They had to make the LORD the object of their faith. If they had refused to believe the promises God gave them through Moses, they would have remained in bondage. In the same way, we have to place our trust in God to take us to Heaven. We have to believe the promises of Jesus. There is no other way. Placing our trust in anything or anyone else will leave us in slavery.

Why Does God Require Faith in Him for Salvation?

The idea that faith in God is necessary to get to Heaven may seem offensive and exclusionary, especially in today's "tolerant" and pluralistic society, but that is mainly because, as a culture, we misunderstand the nature of salvation. We think that traveling to Heaven is about creating a path that we like or that "works best for us." We seem to think that we can build a personal bridge to the Promised Land as we go along, or, to put it another way, blaze our own unique trail. This is simply to misconstrue reality. It is to ignore the fact that Heaven is an objective place and objective places cannot be reached just any old way. To get to a particular place, one must know where, factually, that place is, and where, factually, you are. Then you must travel the appropriate direction using appropriate ways and means.

For example, if I want to get to Seattle and I live in Los Angeles, there is no point in traveling east, as much as I might want to or as much as I think that traveling east would "work best for me." If I travel east from Los Angeles, I will never arrive in Seattle. The reason is, of course, that Seattle and Los Angeles are objective places on an objectively round planet and Seattle lies north of Los Angeles. I must go the right direction if I want to make it.

Veridical guidance isn't the only thing I need, though. Even with the proper directions, I must also have the ability to make the journey. I need resources (vehicles, money, strong legs to walk, etc.) to enable the trip. A good map won't help me if I don't have the power to follow it.

This is the nature of objective travel. It requires knowing the way and having the ability to make the journey. Because Heaven is an objective place, in order to get there we must know the way and also have the ability to make the trip. This is where God comes in. He revealed the only way and only he has the ability to get us there.

In the case of the Israelites, God revealed that they had to go out of Egypt under the blood of the lamb. The Israelites couldn't have made up directions on their own; they had to submit to the reality of the objective situation. Also, only God had the power to defeat Pharaoh and the gods of Egypt, and then, as we will see throughout the rest of the book, get the Israelites across the wilderness. The Hebrews did not have the ability to make it without God.

In the same way, the only way to freedom for us is under the blood of Jesus. We do not have the prerogative to decide that we would rather not go this way. We must submit to objective reality. Also, only God has the power to defeat the enemies that enslave us, and only God has the ability to lead us across the wilderness to the Promised Land. No one but Jesus could defeat Satan and the demons of this world and only Jesus can lead us safely down the narrow road to Heaven.

God requires faith in him to get to Heaven because only he knows the way and only he has the ability to get us there. It is fruitless to place our faith in someone or something that cannot bring about our goal. Giving a dog a paintbrush and trusting it to create the Mona Lisa shows misplaced faith. More to our point, getting directions from someone who doesn't know the land is a waste of time, as is trying to fly a Volkswagen Beetle to the moon. The object of our faith must have the knowledge and ability to accomplish the desired goal. In regards to getting to Heaven, God, and only God, has both.

How Do We Know Where We Are Placing Our Faith? Two Test Questions

Because having faith in God is so important, we must be aware who or what we are trusting. We must always know the object or objects of our faith. We want to always be sure that we are actually following God's directions and relying on his strength.

The problem with this self-examination is that we are notoriously easy on ourselves. "Of course I am trusting God for my future," we might say, as we stress over how the month-end bills are going to get paid or how our retirement plan is doing. Because we tend to rationalize away or simply ignore our lack of true saving faith, the journey to the Promised Land includes some tests. For our own good, God graciously puts us in situations designed to reveal whether we are living by faith in him or by faith in something else.

These situations tell us what we need to know by answering two questions regarding an object of potentially misplaced faith: "How do you react when you don't have it?" and "Are you willing to give it up when you do have it?" The next section of the Exodus story provides a good example of how this works.

Trusting in God or Manna?

After the amazing victory at the Red Sea, God started leading the Israelites across the desert. Even after all they had witnessed, the Israelites soon start to question God's power and goodness.

> Then Moses led Israel from the Red Sea and they went into the Desert of Shur. For three days they traveled in the desert without finding water. When they came to Marah, they could not drink its water because it was bitter. (That is why the place is called Marah.) So the people grumbled against Moses, saying, "What are we to drink?"
>
> Then Moses cried out to the LORD, and the LORD showed him a piece of wood. He threw it into the water, and the water became sweet.
>
> There the LORD made a decree and a law for them, and there he tested them. He said, "If you listen carefully to the voice of the LORD your God and do what is right in his eyes, if you pay attention to his commands and keep all his decrees, I will not bring on you any of the diseases I brought on the Egyptians, for I am the LORD, who heals you."
>
> Then they came to Elim, where there were twelve springs and seventy palm trees, and they camped there near the water.

The whole Israelite community set out from Elim and
came to the Desert of Sin, which is between Elim and
Sinai, on the fifteenth day of the second month after
they had come out of Egypt. In the desert the whole
community grumbled against Moses and Aaron. The
Israelites said to them, "If only we had died by the
LORD's hand in Egypt! There we sat around pots of
meat and ate all the food we wanted, but you have
brought us out into this desert to starve this entire
assembly to death."

Then the LORD said to Moses, "I will rain down
bread from heaven for you. The people are to go out
each day and gather enough for that day. In this way
I will test them and see whether they will follow my
instructions. On the sixth day they are to prepare
what they bring in, and that is to be twice as much as
they gather on the other days."

So Moses and Aaron said to all the Israelites, "In the
evening you will know that it was the LORD who
brought you out of Egypt, and in the morning you
will see the glory of the LORD, because he has heard
your grumbling against him. Who are we, that you
should grumble against us?" Moses also said, "You
will know that it was the LORD when he gives you
meat to eat in the evening and all the bread you want
in the morning, because he has heard your grumbling
against him. Who are we? You are not grumbling
against us, but against the LORD."

Then Moses told Aaron, "Say to the entire Israelite
community, 'Come before the LORD, for he has
heard your grumbling.'"

While Aaron was speaking to the whole Israelite community, they looked toward the desert, and there was the glory of the LORD appearing in the cloud.

The LORD said to Moses, "I have heard the grumbling of the Israelites. Tell them, 'At twilight you will eat meat, and in the morning you will be filled with bread. Then you will know that I am the LORD your God.'"

That evening quail came and covered the camp, and in the morning there was a layer of dew around the camp. When the dew was gone, thin flakes like frost on the ground appeared on the desert floor. When the Israelites saw it, they said to each other, "What is it?" For they did not know what it was.

Moses said to them, "It is the bread the LORD has given you to eat. This is what the LORD has commanded: 'Each one is to gather as much as he needs. Take an omer for each person you have in your tent.'"

The Israelites did as they were told; some gathered much, some little. And when they measured it by the omer, he who gathered much did not have too much, and he who gathered little did not have too little. Each one gathered as much as he needed.

Then Moses said to them, "No one is to keep any of it until morning."

However, some of them paid no attention to Moses; they kept part of it until morning, but it was full of maggots and began to smell. So Moses was angry with them.

Each morning everyone gathered as much as he needed, and when the sun grew hot, it melted away. On the sixth day, they gathered twice as much – two omers for each person – and the leaders of the community came and reported this to Moses. He said to them, "This is what the LORD commanded: 'Tomorrow is to be a day of rest, a holy Sabbath to the LORD. So bake what you want to bake and boil what you want to boil. Save whatever is left and keep it until morning.'"

So they saved it until morning, as Moses commanded, and it did not stink or get maggots in it. "Eat it today," Moses said, "because today is a Sabbath to the LORD. You will not find any of it on the ground today. Six days you are to gather it, but on the seventh day, the Sabbath, there will not be any."

Nevertheless, some of the people went out on the seventh day to gather it, but they found none. Then the LORD said to Moses, "How long will you refuse to keep my commands and my instructions? Bear in mind that the LORD has given you the Sabbath; that is why on the sixth day he gives you bread for two days. Everyone is to stay where he is on the seventh day; no one is to go out." So the people rested on the seventh day.

The people of Israel called the bread manna. It was white like coriander seed and tasted like wafers made with honey. Moses said, "This is what the LORD has commanded: 'Take an omer of manna and keep it for the generations to come, so they can see the bread I gave you to eat in the desert when I brought you out of Egypt.'"

So Moses said to Aaron, "Take a jar and put an omer of manna in it. Then place it before the LORD to be kept for the generations to come."

As the LORD commanded Moses, Aaron put the manna in front of the Testimony, that it might be kept. The Israelites ate manna forty years, until they came to a land that was settled; they ate manna until they reached the border of Canaan. (Exodus 15:22-16:35)

God took his people out into the desert to test them. He wanted to reveal whether or not they were actually making him the object of their faith. Unfortunately, many were not. They were not trusting in his guidance or provision. We know this because they answered both of the test questions incorrectly.

In this instance, the people were placing their trust the proverbial "bird in the hand." Some of their security obviously came from full plates and pantries because as soon as they didn't have these things, they whined and complained and were convinced they were going to die Even as slaves, it seems they never lacked for food or water in Egypt (Exodus 16:3). Their trust in food stocks was revealed as soon as God took them away.

In the second part of the test, God miraculously provided them food, but then told them not to hoard it. They were to gather only enough manna for one day (except on the day before the Sabbath, when they could get enough for two days) because God would provide what they needed again the next day. By asking the Israelites to give up the cache of food, God was saying, in effect, "Do you trust me or do you trust a storage tent full of manna? What is the object of your faith?" The people who answered by stockpiling the food showed that they were trusting in the manna.

Misplaced Faith in Money and Things

While we probably are not tempted to literally hoard food as a guarantee for the future, this story does speak clearly to our tendency to trust in money and possessions. Perhaps the premier object of misplaced faith in all of creation is stuff. As such, God often uses the two test questions to reveal whether or not we are trusting in riches.

For example, God tested Job by taking away almost everything he had (Job 1:6-2:7). When confronted with the question "What do you do when a potential object of misplaced faith is taken away?" Job's wife encouraged him to "curse God and die" (Job 2:9). Doing so would have proved that Job had been putting his faith in riches (among other things, perhaps.) He didn't curse God because he had not been trusting in his riches. He even pointed this out as part of his defense before God.

> If I have put my trust in gold or said to pure gold, 'You are my security,' if I have rejoiced over my great wealth, the fortune my hands had gained, if I have regarded the sun in its radiance or the moon moving in splendor, so that my heart was secretly enticed and my hand offered them a kiss of homage, then these also would be sins to be judged, for I would have been unfaithful to God on high. (Job 31:24-28).

Job passed the test. When faced with the absence of riches, he did not despair because riches were not the object of his faith. Rather, his hope for the future was placed in

God: "I know that my Redeemer lives, and that in the end he will stand upon the earth. And after my skin has been destroyed, yet in my flesh I will see God; I myself will see him with my own eyes – I, and not another. How my heart yearns within me!" (Job 19:25-27).

If only the rich young ruler had done as well with his test. As we revisit this story, remember that this man came to Jesus and asked what was needed to inherit eternal life. Jesus told him to keep the commandments.

"Teacher," he declared, "all these I have kept since I was a boy."

Jesus looked at him and loved him. "One thing you lack," he said. "Go, sell everything you have and give to the poor, and you will have treasure in heaven. Then come, follow me."

At this the man's face fell. He went away sad, because he had great wealth.

Jesus looked around and said to his disciples, "How hard it is for the rich to enter the kingdom of God!"

The disciples were amazed at his words. But Jesus said again, "Children, how hard it is to enter the kingdom of God! It is easier for a camel to go through the eye of a needle than for a rich man to enter the kingdom of God."

The disciples were even more amazed, and said to each other, "Who then can be saved?"

Jesus looked at them and said, "With man this is impossible, but not with God; all things are possible with God."

Peter said to him, "We have left everything to follow you!"

"I tell you the truth," Jesus replied, "no one who has left home or brothers or sisters or mother or father or children or fields for me and the gospel will fail to receive a hundred times as much in this present age (homes, brothers, sisters, mothers, children and fields – and with them, persecutions) and in the age to come, eternal life. But many who are first will be last, and the last first." (Mark 10:20-31)

Jesus reveals that the man is placing his faith in wealth by asking him to give it up. The man could not. On the other hand, the disciples had demonstrated that Jesus was the object of their faith by giving up everything and following him. In the end, Jesus assures them, they will be rewarded, while all those who trust in riches will get nothing but punishment. Everyone will reap what they have sown. The Psalmist teaches the same lesson in prophesying about the man who trusts in riches.

Surely God will bring you down to everlasting ruin: He will snatch you up and tear you from your tent; he will uproot you from the land of the living. *Selah*

The righteous will see and fear; they will laugh at him, saying, "Here now is the man who did not make God his stronghold but trusted in his great wealth and grew strong by destroying others!" (Psalm 52:5-7)

Jesus reiterated the futility of trusting in material possessions when he was asked to mediate a dispute over money.

> Someone in the crowd said to him, "Teacher, tell my
> brother to divide the inheritance with me."

> Jesus replied, "Man, who appointed me a judge or an
> arbiter between you?" Then he said to them, "Watch
> out! Be on your guard against all kinds of greed; a
> man's life does not consist in the abundance of his
> possessions."

> And he told them this parable: "The ground of a
> certain rich man produced a good crop. He thought
> to himself, 'What shall I do? I have no place to store
> my crops.'

> "Then he said, 'This is what I'll do. I will tear down
> my barns and build bigger ones, and there I will store
> all my grain and my goods. And I'll say to myself,
> "You have plenty of good things laid up for many
> years. Take life easy; eat, drink and be merry."'

> "But God said to him, 'You fool! This very night
> your life will be demanded from you. Then who will
> get what you have prepared for yourself?'

> "This is how it will be with anyone who stores up
> things for himself but is not rich toward God." (Luke
> 12:13-21)

You Can't Take It With You

While money may seem like a solid investment in the
future, it's not hard to see why it should not be trusted. As

the old adage says, you simply can't take it with you. Money may be helpful for achieving some benefits here on earth, but it is entirely useless at securing the one thing we really need: eternal life with God. At the end of the day, money cannot buy one square inch of property in the Promised Land. As Jesus said, "What good is it for a man to gain the whole world, yet forfeit his soul?" (Mark 8:36). Because of this, the Bible is unequivocal in warning against trusting in riches.

> If anyone teaches false doctrines and does not agree to the sound instruction of our Lord Jesus Christ and to godly teaching, he is conceited and understands nothing. He has an unhealthy interest in controversies and quarrels about words that result in envy, strife, malicious talk, evil suspicions and constant friction between men of corrupt mind, who have been robbed of the truth and who think that godliness is a means to financial gain.

> But godliness with contentment is great gain. For we brought nothing into the world, and we can take nothing out of it. But if we have food and clothing, we will be content with that. People who want to get rich fall into temptation and a trap and into many foolish and harmful desires that plunge men into ruin and destruction. For the love of money is a root of all kinds of evil. Some people, eager for money, have wandered from the faith and pierced themselves with many griefs. ...

> Command those who are rich in this present world not to be arrogant nor to put their hope in wealth, which is so uncertain, but to put their hope in God, who richly provides us with everything for our enjoyment. Command them to do good, to be rich in good deeds,

and to be generous and willing to share. In this way they will lay up treasure for themselves as a firm foundation for the coming age, so that they may take hold of the life that is truly life. (1 Tim 6:3-10; 17-19)

Again, Paul was just echoing the teachings of Jesus:

Do not store up for yourselves treasures on earth, where moth and rust destroy, and where thieves break in and steal. But store up for yourselves treasures in heaven, where moth and rust do not destroy, and where thieves do not break in and steal. For where your treasure is, there your heart will be also.

The eye is the lamp of the body. If your eyes are good, your whole body will be full of light. But if your eyes are bad, your whole body will be full of darkness. If then the light within you is darkness, how great is that darkness!

No one can serve two masters. Either he will hate the one and love the other, or he will be devoted to the one and despise the other. You cannot serve both God and Money. (Matthew 6:19-24)

Do We Have to Be Paupers?

Some have interpreted Jesus' teaching as an injunction against the possession of any money or things. It is not. Jesus was not saying that money is evil in and of itself, only that we are not to put our faith in it. As long as money serves us rather than us serving it, possessing it is fine. After Job passed the test, he was given back even more possessions than were taken away from him (Job 42:12). As long as we can answer the two test questions correctly, God can trust us with money. We need to be willing to give it up when we have it and not complain about it when we don't. Paul exemplified this in his life. When thanking the church in Philippi for their support of him, Paul explained,

> I am not saying this because I am in need, for I have learned to be content whatever the circumstances. I know what it is to be in need, and I know what it is to have plenty. I have learned the secret of being content in any and every situation, whether well fed or hungry, whether living in plenty or in want. I can do everything through him who gives me strength. (Philippians 4:11-13)

Paul was content with money or without it because the object of his faith was God, not stuff.

All We Need to Carry Out the Mission

"But," you might be thinking, "if I don't have money how will I survive?" Well, just as God provided fresh manna for the Israelites every morning, he will provide you with everything you need to do his will. Just as governments provide their armies with food, weapons, and ammunition, God takes care of the needs of his people. When God sends people into the battle, he does not do so without the equipment and support they need.

After Paul thanked the Philippians for their help, he went on to encourage them in their sacrificial giving by explaining that, just as his needs had been supplied, theirs would be as well. "And my God will meet all your needs according to his glorious riches in Christ Jesus" (Philippians 4:19). Those that seek first the Kingdom of God are provided with all they need to accomplish their task. Because of this, we can rest easy, knowing that God is more faithful and more generous than the best government. Jesus makes this clear.

> Therefore I tell you, do not worry about your life, what you will eat or drink; or about your body, what you will wear. Is not life more important than food, and the body more important than clothes? Look at the birds of the air; they do not sow or reap or store away in barns, and yet your heavenly Father feeds them. Are you not much more valuable than they? Who of you by worrying can add a single hour to his life?
>
> And why do you worry about clothes? See how the lilies of the field grow. They do not labor or spin. Yet I tell you that not even Solomon in all his splendor was dressed like one of these. If that is how God clothes the grass of the field, which is here today and tomorrow is thrown into the fire, will he not much more clothe you, O you of little faith? So do not worry, saying, "What shall we eat?" or "What shall we drink?" or "What shall we wear?" For the pagans run after all these things, and your heavenly Father knows that you need them. But seek first his kingdom and his righteousness, and all these things will be given to you as well. Therefore do not worry about tomorrow, for tomorrow will worry about itself. Each day has enough trouble of its own. (Matthew 6:25-34)

Other Objects of False Trust

Of course money is not the only thing in which we wrongly place our trust. In the Bible one of the more common objects of misplaced trust is military might. Israel and the other nations were often found guilty of putting their hope in strong armies rather than God. Unfortunately, the strength of soldiers and horses is just as useless at guaranteeing the future as riches. Thankfully, there were a couple of leaders who understood this. God exposed their faith with the same test he applies to riches. Regarding military strength, he asked them, "How do you react when you don't have it?" and "Are you willing to give it up?"

King Jehoshaphat passed the test wonderfully. He did not have a large army, so when faced with an attacking military alliance of three strong nations, he called for a day of prayer and fasting. In doing so, he affirmed his trust in God.

> After this, the Moabites and Ammonites with some of the Meunites came to make war on Jehoshaphat. Some men came and told Jehoshaphat, "A vast army is coming against you from Edom, from the other side of the Sea. It is already in Hazazon Tamar" (that is, En Gedi). Alarmed, Jehoshaphat resolved to inquire of the LORD, and he proclaimed a fast for all Judah. The people of Judah came together to seek help from the LORD; indeed, they came from every town in Judah to seek him.
>
> Then Jehoshaphat stood up in the assembly of Judah and Jerusalem at the temple of the LORD in the front of the new courtyard and said: "O LORD, God of our fathers, are you not the God who is in heaven? You rule over all the kingdoms of the nations. Power and might are in your hand, and no one can withstand you. O our God, did you not drive out the inhabitants of this land before your people Israel and give it forever to the descendants of Abraham your friend? They have lived in it and have built in it a sanctuary for your Name, saying, 'If calamity comes upon us, whether the sword of judgment, or plague or famine,

we will stand in your presence before this temple that bears your Name and will cry out to you in our distress, and you will hear us and save us.'

"But now here are men from Ammon, Moab and Mount Seir, whose territory you would not allow Israel to invade when they came from Egypt; so they turned away from them and did not destroy them. See how they are repaying us by coming to drive us out of the possession you gave us as an inheritance. O our God, will you not judge them? For we have no power to face this vast army that is attacking us. We do not know what to do, but our eyes are upon you." (2 Chronicles 20:1-12)

Jehoshaphat passed his test with flying colors, and God provided him with a miraculous victory. Jehoshaphat was making God the object of his faith rather than military might and he showed this by reacting properly when he lacked those forces.

God also tested the faith of another military leader of Israel, although in this case the situation was reversed. Rather than being in a position of weakness and defense, Gideon was preparing his strong army to attack some weaker enemies. Then God stepped in and asked Gideon to send some of the soldiers home. God wanted to see what Gideon would do when asked to give up a potential object of his faith.

Early in the morning, Jerub-Baal (that is, Gideon) and all his men camped at the spring of Harod. The camp of Midian was north of them in the valley near the hill of Moreh. The LORD said to Gideon, "You have too many men for me to deliver Midian into their hands. In order that Israel may not boast against me that her own strength has saved her, announce now to the people, 'Anyone who trembles with fear may turn back and leave Mount Gilead.'" So twenty-two thousand men left, while ten thousand remained.

But the LORD said to Gideon, "There are still too many men. Take them down to the water, and I will sift them for you there. If I say, 'This one shall go with you,' he shall go; but if I say, 'This one shall not go with you,' he shall not go."

So Gideon took the men down to the water. There the LORD told him, "Separate those who lap the water with their tongues like a dog from those who kneel down to drink." Three hundred men lapped with their hands to their mouths. All the rest got down on their knees to drink.

The LORD said to Gideon, "With the three hundred men that lapped I will save you and give the Midianites into your hands. Let all the other men go, each to his own place." So Gideon sent the rest of the Israelites to their tents but kept the three hundred, who took over the provisions and trumpets of the others. (Judges 7:1-8)

Just like Jehoshaphat, Gideon passed the test, and God granted him a huge military victory. These two rulers lived out the words of the song of David: "Some trust in chariots and some in horses, but we trust in the name of the LORD our God" (Psalm 20:7). In doing so they avoided the curse of Isaiah: "Woe to those who go down to Egypt for help, who rely on horses, who trust in the multitude of their chariots and in the great strength of their horsemen, but do not look to the Holy One of Israel, or seek help from the LORD" (Isaiah 31:1).

The Futility of Self-Confidence

Unless you are a high ranking officer in the military, I suspect the last couple of examples may seem inapplicable. However, I think the biblical teaching on trust in military might can be applied to our temptation to trust human strength in general.

We love to base our confidence in ourselves. Indeed, self-confidence is encouraged. "Believe in yourself" has become an unquestioned mantra in our society. From faith in intellectual abilities to trust in physical prowess, self has become one of the premier objects of idolatry. However, faith in self is just as misplaced as faith in money or weapons. We can no more secure our own future and get ourselves to the Promised Land than we can fly ourselves to the surface of the sun. Self-confidence is a recipe for disaster.

According to Proverbs, "Pride goes before destruction, a haughty spirit before a fall" (Proverbs 16:18). "Do you see a man wise in his own eyes? There is more hope for a fool than for him" (Proverbs 26:12). Isaiah expands on these warnings by clarifying what will happen.

> The arrogance of man will be brought low and the pride of men humbled; the LORD alone will be exalted in that day, and the idols will totally disappear. Men will flee to caves in the rocks and to holes in the ground from dread of the LORD and the splendor of his majesty, when he rises to shake the earth.
>
> In that day men will throw away to the rodents and bats their idols of silver and idols of gold, which they made to worship.
>
> They will flee to caverns in the rocks and to the overhanging crags from dread of the LORD and the

splendor of his majesty, when he rises to shake the earth.

Stop trusting in man, who has but a breath in his nostrils. Of what account is he? (Isaiah 2:17-22)

He summarizes a few chapters later, "Woe to those who are wise in their own eyes and clever in their own sight" (Isaiah 5:21).
Jeremiah adds to the prophetic charge by comparing those who trust in God with those who trust in themselves.

This is what the LORD says: "Cursed is the one who trusts in man, who depends on flesh for his strength and whose heart turns away from the LORD.

He will be like a bush in the wastelands; he will not see prosperity when it comes. He will dwell in the parched places of the desert, in a salt land where no one lives.

"But blessed is the man who trusts in the LORD, whose confidence is in him. He will be like a tree planted by the water that sends out its roots by the stream. It does not fear when heat comes; its leaves are always green. It has no worries in a year of drought and never fails to bear fruit." (Jeremiah 17:5-8)

Here is the bottom line: "It is better to take refuge in the LORD than to trust in man. It is better to take refuge in the LORD than to trust in princes" (Psalm 118:8-9). As part of the discussion in the next section, we will see a few examples of people who had their misplaced confidence exposed by God.

Not a Typical Test

So God wants us to make him the sole object of our faith, and he places us in situations to test to see if we are doing that. By revealing how we react when we lack certain things or are asked to give them up, God shows us if we are trusting him or if we are trusting something else.

It should be noted here that this is not a typical test. God's tests are set up to be passed – they are stacked in our favor. At least in the instance of God taking something away, the act of going through the test should actually help us arrive at the correct answer. Here is how it works.

When God takes something away from us, not only is he testing to expose whether or not we are going to complain, but he is teaching us that we have no reason to complain because we don't really need that thing. When we survive and even thrive without whatever it is in which we were trusting, we should see the futility of trusting in that thing and therefore not complain. This is something we probably would not have known if it had never been taken away.

According to Deuteronomy 8:2, God sent the people into the desert without food to humble them as well as test them. By taking away their food, God was testing the Israelites to see how they would react, but he was also trying to teach them that "man does not live on bread alone but on every word that comes from the mouth of the LORD." He intended to break down their trust in stuff by taking that stuff away.

God has graciously used this testing and humbling process many times in my own life. As a 21 year old, I was the epitome of foolish self-confidence. I really felt like I had life by the tail and could do whatever I wanted with it. That ended one cold spring night on the Canadian plains. My good friend and I were driving home from playing hockey in southern Saskatchewan when we crossed a bridge covered in "black" (extremely transparent) ice. My short-box pickup truck skidded out of control and flipped over several times. I was thrown through the driver's side window. The next thing I remember is waking up in a hospital bed, unable to move.

The brush with death had a clarifying effect on me. As I lay paralyzed, I realized that I had been arrogant and foolish and that all I had been chasing after in life – money, stuff, fun experiences – was a complete waste of time. At that moment, all I wanted to do was get right with God, so I repented of my stupidity and misplaced faith and surrendered my life to his service.

God humbled me by taking away my health (at least briefly – I had no major injuries and was walking the next day), my truck, and almost my life. He put me through a test and, although I was not putting my faith in him as I entered the test, by the end I was. The act of going through the test had helped me pass it.

God did something similar with King Nebuchadnezzar. As ruler of Babylon, he had everything going for him. Unfortunately, he got full of himself, so God humbled him by taking everything away.

> All this happened to King Nebuchadnezzar. Twelve months later, as the king was walking on the roof of the royal palace of Babylon, he said, "Is not this the great Babylon I have built as the royal residence, by my mighty power and for the glory of my majesty?"

> The words were still on his lips when a voice came from heaven, "This is what is decreed for you, King Nebuchadnezzar: Your royal authority has been taken from you. You will be driven away from people and will live with the wild animals; you will eat grass like cattle. Seven times will pass by for you until you acknowledge that the Most High is sovereign over the kingdoms of men and gives them to anyone he wishes."

Immediately what had been said about Nebuchadnezzar was fulfilled. He was driven away from people and ate grass like cattle. His body was drenched with the dew of heaven until his hair grew like the feathers of an eagle and his nails like the claws of a bird.

At the end of that time, I, Nebuchadnezzar, raised my eyes toward heaven, and my sanity was restored. Then I praised the Most High; I honored and glorified him who lives forever. His dominion is an eternal dominion; his kingdom endures from generation to generation.

All the peoples of the earth are regarded as nothing. He does as he pleases with the powers of heaven and the peoples of the earth. No one can hold back his hand or say to him: "What have you done?"

At the same time that my sanity was restored, my honor and splendor were returned to me for the glory of my kingdom. My advisers and nobles sought me out, and I was restored to my throne and became even greater than before. Now I, Nebuchadnezzar, praise and exalt and glorify the King of heaven, because everything he does is right and all his ways are just. And those who walk in pride he is able to humble. (Daniel 4:28-34)

Concluding Thoughts on Faith and Testing

Before leaving this subject, I want to conclude this chapter with a couple of points. First, testing will not always bring humility. Although my testing experience resulted in repentance, it is conceivable that my heart could have hardened instead. I could have got angry at God for allowing such a thing to happen. Not everyone will pass the test. I am sure we all know people who harbor a grudge against God for some harm they think he has caused them in the past. Traveling through the wilderness can result in hard hearts as well as soft, as we will see in later chapters. Paul contrasts "godly sorrow," which leads to repentance and "worldly sorrow," which does not (2 Corinthians 7:9-11). The correct response to a test is humility, not greater pride.

Second, humbling and testing is not a one-time event. Pride rears its ugly head often, and God will continue to put us in tough situations in an attempt to keep us humble.

Not long after I surrendered my life on that hospital bed, I found myself working with inner-city kids at a summer camp in Northern California. As a farm boy from Canada, this was a bit out of my comfort zone. However, I went in with confidence that I had the strength to do it. After all, I was a tough Canadian, right? That was a big mistake.

The camp ran for nine weeks and by week six and seven most of the workers were exhausted and longing to be done. I, however, still felt good and was starting to look down at the "weaklings" I was working with. Then, in week eight, I received what I am sure is still considered to be the worst cabin of boys in the history of Camp May Mac. These guys were the toughest, brattiest kids I had ever met, and I had eight of them. It was simply too much. One day while walking down to the dining hall, I finally snapped. It is not that anything especially bad or out of the ordinary happened – just one more vulgar comment about me and my mother, as far as I remember – but it was the last straw. I grabbed one of the boys by the shirt and lifted him off the ground. His eyes got really big, and I could see that he felt I might really harm him. Then it hit me: *I* felt I might really harm him. I quickly dropped him to the ground, handed my group off to another counselor, and went into the woods. There I literally cried out to God, "I can't do this."

"Exactly," was God's response. "It is about time you understood that. You *can't* do this, at least not in your own strength. Trusting in yourself is going to get you nowhere. Put your faith in me."

Tough circumstances are designed not only to test us, but to humble us and enable us to come out of the test with a passing grade. I had become proud, and God had to take away my strength in order to humble me. God will send these tests as often as we need them, a fact Paul celebrated:

> To keep me from becoming conceited because of these surpassingly great revelations, there was given me a thorn in my flesh, a messenger of Satan, to torment me. Three times I pleaded with the Lord to take it away from me. But he said to me, "My grace is sufficient for you, for my power is made perfect in weakness." Therefore I will boast all the more gladly about my weaknesses, so that Christ's power may rest on me. That is why, for Christ's sake, I delight in weaknesses, in insults, in hardships, in persecutions, in difficulties. For when I am weak, then I am strong. (2 Corinthians 12:7-10)

By God's grace we are saved through faith in Him. Only he knows the way to the Promised Land and only he has the ability to get us there. Because of this, he must be the sole object of our faith. As such, God will do everything he can to cause us to trust in him and to keep us trusting in him. He sends us into the wilderness to humble us and test us. May we respond to each test following Paul's example and James' admonition: "Consider it pure joy, my brothers, whenever you face trials of many kinds, because you know that the testing of your faith develops perseverance. Perseverance must finish its work so that you may be mature and complete, not lacking anything" (James 1:2-4).

CHAPTER 7

Work

So Joshua overcame the Amalekite army with the sword.

EXODUS 17:13

Faith by itself, if it is not accompanied by action, is dead.

JAMES 2:17

Work vs. Works

As I emphasized at the beginning of Chapter 6, God is the focus of salvation. All humans have to do is have faith. Seems simple enough, right? We just trust God and enjoy the ride home, basically doing nothing. Well, not quite. There is still human work to be done.

Now here we must tread very carefully, as I am sure many of you are already thinking, "But just last chapter we read Ephesians 2:8: 'For it is by grace you have been saved, through faith – and this not from yourselves, it is the gift of God – not by works, so that no one can boast.'" That is absolutely true. However, that does not mean there is not work to do. You see, there is a difference between working for your salvation and working out your salvation. It is the difference between the works that Paul warns will not save in Ephesians 2 and the work that James assures us must happen in James 2:

> What good is it, my brothers, if a man claims to have faith but has no deeds? Can such faith save him? Suppose a brother or sister is without clothes and daily food. If one of you says to him, "Go, I wish you well; keep warm and well fed," but does nothing about his physical needs, what good is it? In the same way, faith by itself, if it is not accompanied by action, is dead.
>
> But someone will say, "You have faith; I have deeds." Show me your faith without deeds, and I will show you my faith by what I do.
>
> You believe that there is one God. Good! Even the demons believe that – and shudder.
>
> You foolish man, do you want evidence that faith without deeds is useless? Was not our ancestor Abraham considered righteous for what he did when he offered his son Isaac on the altar? You see that his faith and his actions were working together, and his faith was made complete by what he did. And the scripture was fulfilled that says, "Abraham believed God, and it was credited to him as righteousness," and he was called God's friend. You see that a person is justified by what he does and not by faith alone.
>
> In the same way, was not even Rahab the prostitute considered righteous for what she did when she gave

lodging to the spies and sent them off in a different direction? As the body without the spirit is dead, so faith without deeds is dead. (James 2:14-26)

At first glance James seems to contradict Paul. He does not. The key is to understand the difference between works as Paul defined them and works as James defined them. For the purpose of my argument I will refer to Paul's term as "works" and James' term as "work." We are not to do works, but we are to work.

Here are some of the differences between works and work. Works are tasks undertaken for the purpose of raising our own stature. Work is undertaken to raise God's stature. We know we have been doing works if we can look back on them and take pride in our accomplishment. We know we have been working if, when we look back, we see nothing but God's accomplishment. Works are useless at procuring salvation. Work is an absolutely essential part of procuring salvation. We will never get to the Promised Land by doing works, but we will also never get to the Promised Land if we refuse to work.

In this chapter we will look primarily at examples of the righteous work that James commands, and in Chapter 8, as part of our discussion of righteousness, we will examine some examples of the works that Paul condemns.

We Still Have to Swing the Sword

When the Children of Israel survived the Passover, God did not place the blood on the door for them. They had to physically kill a lamb and use hyssop to get the blood in the right place.

When the Israelites were told to leave Egypt, God did not provide them with limousines for the trip across the desert. They had to walk.

When the armies of Egypt were bearing down on the Israelites at the shores of the Red Sea, God did not provide them with ships. God parted the sea and, again, they had to walk.

In each case, do you suppose the Israelites were tempted to look back on their deliverance and say, "Wow, we were great! Look at how we defeated the Egyptians! That was a tremendous display of our own wisdom and power!"? I doubt it. One does not sensibly look back at the Red Sea crossing or the plagues and see anything but God's power and glory. However, does that mean that the Israelites played no part in their own deliverance? No. They still had to slaughter the sheep, place the blood, pack up their belongings and walk. They had to do some work. They did not just sit on the ground and passively wait for God's deliverance. When God told them to act, they acted.

When God provided manna in the wilderness, he did not place it directly in their mouths or in their stomachs. He let it fall on the ground and the people had to go out and gather it. Could they look back on this task with any sort of self-congratulation? Of course not. There was no possibility of them taking credit for feeding themselves in the wilderness. However, if they had not gone out and used their hands to gather food, they would not have eaten, so they did play a part in the process.

This is the kind of work God asks us to do. We are to labor as part of his plan of redemption, but it is not work that will cause us to puff up in pride. It is work done in response to God's grace (God always acts first), in obedience to his command, that results in his glory. Humans work, but they look back on their task and say, "Wow, wasn't God great."

An excellent example of the type of work I am talking about is found in one of the next episodes of the Exodus story:

The Amalekites came and attacked the Israelites at Rephidim. Moses said to Joshua, "Choose some of our men and go out to fight the Amalekites. Tomorrow I will stand on top of the hill with the staff of God in my hands."

So Joshua fought the Amalekites as Moses had ordered, and Moses, Aaron and Hur went to the top of the hill. As long as Moses held up his hands, the Israelites were winning, but whenever he lowered his hands, the Amalekites were winning. When Moses' hands grew tired, they took a stone and put it under him and he sat on it. Aaron and Hur held his hands up – one on one side, one on the other – so that his hands remained steady till sunset. So Joshua overcame the Amalekite army with the sword. (Exodus 17:8-13)

The Israelites had to go to war. They physically had to face the Amalekites in man-to-man combat. However, they could not look back after the victory and take pride in their accomplishment, nor could they stand in awe at their own bravery and strength on the battlefield, because it was clear who won the victory – God.

In allowing the Israelites to prevail in the battle only when Moses' hand was in the air, God showed who was in charge of the fight. The victory was all God, yet the soldiers of Israel still had to go out and swing their swords. They had to work to defeat the Amalekites, but even while pouring out their own sweat and blood, all the glory for the victory had to go to God.

By Faith They Worked

This is the type of work we need to be doing. We need to be sweating for the Kingdom, busy about our Father's business, just as Jesus was (John 5:17). As James explained, work is the mark of true faith. There is no such thing as true faith without deeds, just as there is no such thing as righteous deeds without faith. Bonhoeffer wrote, "Only he who believes is obedient, and only he who is obedient believes."[17] One cannot separate faith and action.

Just believing in your head that God exists or even that he is good is not enough. True faith shows itself in deeds. Look at the heroes of faith showcased in Hebrews 11. Without exception, they are people whose faith is described by action. Look at all the verb clauses that accompany the term "by faith" in this passage:

> By faith Abel *offered God a better sacrifice* than Cain did. By faith he was commended as a righteous man, when God spoke well of his offerings. And by faith he still speaks, even though he is dead. ...

> By faith Noah, when warned about things not yet seen, in holy fear *built an ark* to save his family. By his faith he *condemned the world* and became heir of the righteousness that comes by faith.

> By faith Abraham, when called to go to a place he would later receive as his inheritance, *obeyed and went*, even though he did not know where he was going. By faith he *made his home* in the promised land like a stranger in a foreign country; he lived in tents, as did Isaac and Jacob, who were heirs with him of the same promise. For he was looking forward to the city with foundations, whose architect and builder is God. ...

> By faith Abraham, when God tested him, *offered Isaac* as a sacrifice. He who had received the promises was

about to sacrifice his one and only son, even though God had said to him, "It is through Isaac that your offspring will be reckoned." Abraham reasoned that God could raise the dead, and figuratively speaking, he did receive Isaac back from death.

By faith Isaac *blessed Jacob and Esau* in regard to their future.

By faith Jacob, when he was dying, *blessed each of Joseph's sons*, and worshiped as he leaned on the top of his staff.

By faith Joseph, when his end was near, *spoke about the exodus* of the Israelites from Egypt and gave instructions about his bones.

By faith Moses' parents *hid him for three months* after he was born, because they saw he was no ordinary child, and they were not afraid of the king's edict.

By faith Moses, when he had grown up, *refused to be known* as the son of Pharaoh's daughter. He *chose to be mistreated* along with the people of God rather than to enjoy the pleasures of sin for a short time. He regarded disgrace for the sake of Christ as of greater value than the treasures of Egypt, because he was looking ahead to his reward. By faith he *left Egypt*, not fearing the king's anger; he persevered because he saw him who is invisible. By faith he *kept the Passover* and the sprinkling of blood, so that the destroyer of the firstborn would not touch the firstborn of Israel.

By faith the people *passed through the Red Sea* as on dry land; but when the Egyptians tried to do so, they were drowned.

By faith the walls of Jericho fell, after the people had *marched around them for seven days.*

By faith the prostitute Rahab, because she *welcomed the spies*, was not killed with those who were disobedient.

And what more shall I say? I do not have time to tell about Gideon, Barak, Samson, Jephthah, David, Samuel and the prophets, who through faith *conquered kingdoms, administered justice, and gained what was promised; who shut the mouths of lions, quenched the fury of the flames, and escaped the edge of the sword; whose weakness was turned to strength; and who became powerful in battle and routed foreign armies.* Women received back their dead, raised to life again. Others were tortured and *refused to be released*, so that they might gain a better resurrection. Some faced jeers and flogging, while still others were chained and put in prison. They were stoned; they were sawed in two; they were put to death by the sword. They *went about in sheepskins and goatskins*, destitute, persecuted and mistreated – the world was not worthy of them. They *wandered in deserts and mountains*, and in caves and holes in the ground.

These were all commended for their faith, yet none of them received what had been promised. God had planned something better for us so that only together with us would they be made perfect. (Hebrews 4:4, 7-10, 17-40, emphasis mine)

What a tremendous example for us! Look back over the list of works. Notice in each case that the task was undertaken out of obedience to God and resulted in glory to God. Not one of these heroes of faith would look back on what they did with a sense of pride. How could they? Obedience to God results in a display of his power that is unmistakable.

That is why Goliath was defeated by a shepherd boy using stones (1 Samuel 17:48-50). If the Israelites had won using regular soldiers and weapons, they may have been tempted to think that their own strength had saved them. That is why Jericho was defeated by marching and trumpet blasts rather than a battering ram (Joshua 6:20). Nobody could question that God had brought the walls down. However, in each case God's servants had to obediently do *something*. David had to pick out some stones and swing the sling. Joshua and his people had to walk around Jericho for seven days. It was not a case of simply assenting to some proposition about God's power or being passive receptacles in some other way – they actually had to put their money where their mouth was, so to speak.

The story is often told about a man who was walking a tightrope across Niagara Falls. Here is a typical version:

> A crowd gathered and cheered the man on. The man faced the crowd and said, "How many of you think that I can push this empty wheelbarrow across Niagara Falls on the tightrope?" The crowd cheered wildly in support. The man successfully pushed the wheelbarrow across the falls and back. Then, the man said, "How many of you think I can push a wheelbarrow full of bricks across Niagara Falls?" The crowd went crazy, encouraging the man to try. As expected, the man successfully pushed the wheelbarrow full of bricks across Niagara Falls and back. Finally, the man turned to the crowd and said, "How many of you

think that I can push another person in this wheel-barrow across Niagara Falls?" The people cheered, jumping up and down and screaming to see this feat. The man then said, "Who would like to volunteer?"

The crowd fell deathly silent. Not one person who claimed to believe in the tightrope walker was willing to trust him with his/her own life.[18]

Faith that does not produce action is no faith at all.

Obedience vs. Testing

Now, I want to emphasize that actions are not righteous in and of themselves. They must be done in obedience to God and for his glory. There is no point in literally setting up a tightrope across Niagara Falls so you can ride across in wheel-barrow to show your trust. God will provide opportunities to step out in faith. Trying to create those opportunities on your own puts the focus on your "faith" rather than God's power. In those situations you are seeking your own glory rather than God's. Even though you are ostensibly relying on God's power, what you are really saying is, "I am special – look at how much faith I have." If you are not acting in obedience to God, it turns into an act of testing him. This is to be avoided. God tests you, you don't test God. Satan tried to get Jesus to test God by jumping off the highest point of the temple:

Then the devil took [Jesus] to the holy city and had him stand on the highest point of the temple. "If you are the Son of God," he said, "throw yourself down. For it is written: 'He will command his angels concerning you, and they will lift you up in their hands, so that you will not strike your foot against a stone.'"

Jesus answered him, "It is also written: 'Do not put the Lord your God to the test.'"(Matthew 4:5-7)

Satan tried to get Jesus to verify his special standing as the Son of God by getting God the Father to do a miracle for him. The focus was on Jesus, not God. Jesus rightly refused and supported his decision by quoting Deuteronomy 6:16: "Do not test the LORD your God as you did at Massah." This is a reference to an incident from the Exodus that occurred just before the battle with the Amalekites:

> The whole Israelite community set out from the Desert of Sin, traveling from place to place as the LORD commanded. They camped at Rephidim, but there was no water for the people to drink. So they quarreled with Moses and said, "Give us water to drink."
>
> Moses replied, "Why do you quarrel with me? Why do you put the LORD to the test?"
>
> But the people were thirsty for water there, and they grumbled against Moses. They said, "Why did you bring us up out of Egypt to make us and our children and livestock die of thirst?"
>
> Then Moses cried out to the LORD, "What am I to do with these people? They are almost ready to stone me."
>
> The LORD answered Moses, "Walk on ahead of the people. Take with you some of the elders of Israel and take in your hand the staff with which you struck the Nile, and go. I will stand there before you by the rock at Horeb. Strike the rock, and water will come

out of it for the people to drink." So Moses did this in the sight of the elders of Israel. And he called the place Massah and Meribah because the Israelites quarreled and because they tested the LORD saying, "Is the LORD among us or not?" (Exodus 17:1-7)

The key to understanding this story (and why Jesus refers to it) is the question, "Is the LORD among us or not?" The Israelites were thirsty and appealed to God (through Moses) to do a miracle for them. But notice the nature of this appeal. In asking if the LORD was among them, they were not questioning the existence of God or even whether or not he had the power to provide water. They were asking, "Are we special people or not? Are we God's chosen family or not? Is he among us in a unique way or not?" It was a rhetorical question meant to force God into acting.

The Israelites knew God existed and that he had power to provide water – they had just seen the plagues and the parting of the Red Sea and the miraculous provision of manna. They also knew that they were God's people. He had called and saved just them. When they complained about water, they were asking God to verify that they were special through a miraculous sign. This was the test. In essence they said to God, "Here we are out in the wilderness, trusting only in you. Look at how special we are. Look at our great faith. Now justify that confidence by giving us water."

Jesus would not go down this road. He did not say to God the Father, "Look at me, your one and only son, out here in the desert trusting only in you. I have such great faith that I am willing to jump off this building so that you can rescue me." This would have been testing God, and it is not the type of work God desires.[19]

Interestingly, the incident at Massah provides us with another good example of the type of work God does desire and offers a startling contrast to a later incident when faithful obedience was not practiced. At Massah, God told Moses to strike the rock with his staff and water came out. Moses had something to do, but it was not an action that should result in anything but glory to God. Moses and everyone else understood that, even though Moses struck the rock, God provided the water. Moses' faithful obedience gives us another example of righteous action.

However, if we look a little further ahead in the story, we find the people again grumbling about lack of water. Notice that this time God tells Moses to *speak* to the rock.

> Now there was no water for the community, and the people gathered in opposition to Moses and Aaron. They quarreled with Moses and said, "If only we had died when our brothers fell dead before the LORD! Why did you bring the LORD's community into this desert, that we and our livestock should die here? Why did you bring us up out of Egypt to this terrible place? It has no grain or figs, grapevines or pomegranates. And there is no water to drink!"

> Moses and Aaron went from the assembly to the entrance to the Tent of Meeting and fell facedown, and the glory of the LORD appeared to them. The LORD said to Moses, "Take the staff, and you and your brother Aaron gather the assembly together. Speak to that rock before their eyes and it will pour out its water. You will bring water out of the rock for the community so they and their livestock can drink."

> So Moses took the staff from the LORD's presence, just as he commanded him. He and Aaron gathered the assembly together in front of the rock and Moses said to them, "Listen, you rebels, must we bring you water out of this rock?" Then Moses raised his arm and

145

struck the rock twice with his staff. Water gushed out, and the community and their livestock drank.

But the LORD said to Moses and Aaron, "Because you did not trust in me enough to honor me as holy in the sight of the Israelites, you will not bring this community into the land I give them."

These were the waters of Meribah, where the Israelites quarreled with the LORD and where he showed himself holy among them. (Numbers 20:2-13)

Moses did not obey God's command to speak to the rock. Instead he hit the rock twice with his staff. God saw this as such an egregious lack of faith that he did not allow Moses to enter the Promised Land. At first glance, this might seem a bit harsh. After all, what is the big difference between speaking to the rock and hitting it with a staff? Didn't both actions rely on God's power for success?

Well, not exactly. Notice what Moses said before he hit the rock: "Must *we* bring water out of this rock?" (Deuteronomy 20:10, emphasis mine). Moses did not appeal to God's ability to bring water out of the rock, but his own. Rather than walk in humble obedience to God and follow his command to just speak to the rock, Moses took matters into his own hands. Instead of God getting the glory, Moses took it for himself. Instead of the focus being on God, where it belonged, Moses put the focus on himself. His disobedience was interpreted by God as a lack of faith, which of course lines up with the understanding of faith and works we have been describing. Just as faith always displays itself in obedient action, disobedient action is evidence of a lack of faith.

The Bottom Line

As with running any race or fighting any battle, traveling to the Promised Land requires a lot of hard work. It is not work done in our own strength (which we will talk about in Chapter 10) but it is work nonetheless. God requires obedient action, for this is the nature of true faith. As Paul exhorts and explains, "Therefore, my dear friends, as you have always obeyed – not only in my presence, but now much more in my absence – continue to work out your salvation with fear and trembling, for it is God who works in you to will and to act according to his good purpose" (Philippians 2:12-13).

CHAPTER 8

Rules and Righteousness

For I desire mercy, not sacrifice, and acknowledgment of God rather than burnt offerings.

HOSEA 6:6

But the fruit of the Spirit is love, joy, peace, patience, kindness, goodness, faithfulness, gentleness and self-control. Against such things there is no law.

GALATIANS 5:19-23

Work and Works, Revisited

I wrote in Chapter 7 that we have to work to get to the Promised Land. However, I also mentioned that we must be careful not to do works. I want to expand on the notion of works in this chapter.

It can be hard to distinguish between work and works because the actions performed are often the same. For example, when

Moses struck the rock the first time, he was working. When he struck it the second time, it was works. In both instances, Moses raised his staff and hit the rock. When the Israelites defeated the Amalekites in Exodus 17, they were working, but later, in an episode we will cover in Chapter 13, they went to war against the Canaanites and Amalekites after God had warned them not to and were soundly defeated (Numbers 14:41-45). In both battles the Israelites were swinging their swords, but the first one was work, the second was works. As we will see, it is a person's heart condition that makes something either a work of righteousness or a worthless act of works, not the action itself.

So what does that mean to us? While it is unlikely that we will be asked by God to get water from a rock or take up arms, there are certain activities that are a part of almost every Christian experience. For example, the average Christian life will consist of at least some of the following:

- Attending church services, Bible Studies and other religious functions
- Helping out in some way – doing acts of service within the church and broader community
- Doing outreach and missions work
- Practicing spiritual disciplines such as Bible reading, prayer, study, and fasting
- Giving money to the church and other worthwhile projects

None of these things are inherently wrong. Indeed, one could argue that they are all essential parts of walking the narrow road. Good Christians will practice all of them as part of the righteous work done on the road to Heaven. However, each of these activities can also be practiced as useless works. Instead of being done out of obedience to God and for his honor and glory, they are performed for selfish reasons. Therefore, these activities must be continually evaluated so that we can understand whether they are being performed as work or works. As Jesus warns, even the most apparently successful acts of ministry can be worthless in God's eyes:

> "Not everyone who says to me, 'Lord, Lord,' will enter the kingdom of heaven, but only he who does the will of my Father who is in heaven. Many will say to me on that day, 'Lord, Lord, did we not prophesy in your name, and in your name drive out demons and perform many miracles?' Then I will tell them plainly, 'I never knew you. Away from me, you evil-doers!'" (Matthew 7:21-23)

Jesus is very harsh to these people, even though they had an apparently successful ministry. On the other hand, look at how Jesus responds when his disciples returned from performing exactly the same acts of ministry. After healing people, driving out demons and proclaiming the Kingdom of God (Luke 10:1-16), they were amazed at the power of God.

> The seventy-two returned with joy and said, "Lord, even the demons submit to us in your name."

> He replied, "I saw Satan fall like lightning from heaven. I have given you authority to trample on snakes and scorpions and to overcome all the power of the enemy; nothing will harm you. However, do not rejoice that the spirits submit to you, but rejoice that your names are written in heaven." (Luke 10:17-20)

What was the difference between the miracle workers who got into Heaven and those who didn't? It was not the acts of ministry. There is no indication that the miracles performed in the Matthew 7 passage were counterfeit. Neither was there any problem with the doctrinal beliefs of those doing the ministry. "Lord, Lord" is the proper confession. The people that got cast out were not heretics or hoaxes. The difference between the two groups of people is that, even in the midst of identical outward activities and intellectual assent to the same theological propositions, one was doing the will of God and one was not. Jesus says, "Only he who does the will of my Father who is on Heaven" gets to enter the kingdom.

So, then, what is the will of God? What does God want from us? If you look at the rest of Jesus' sermon (and in particular Matthew 7:15-20, which directly precedes the section we quoted), you will see that God's will in this context is "bearing fruit." So, then, "What is bearing fruit?"

Becoming a Certain Type of Person

Let me start by stating what it is not: bearing fruit is not performing good deeds. It is not taking part in certain activities. Rather, bearing fruit is possessing and exhibiting certain character qualities.

Paul offered a list of these character qualities to the Galatians: "The fruit of the Spirit is love, joy, peace, patience, kindness, goodness, faithfulness, gentleness and self-control. Against such things there is no law" (Galatians 5:22-23). God is interested in making us loving, joyous and peaceful. He wants us to be faithful, gentle, and self-controlled. God's will is that we develop holiness, that we be righteous like him.

This righteousness is a heart condition; it is not performing certain actions. To use our contrasting terms, works are performed so that people might be considered righteous, while work is performed by righteous people. God doesn't want us to do righteous deeds; he wants us to be righteous people.

In emphasizing the importance of distinguishing between a particular act and the type of person performing the act, C.S. Lewis pointed out two dangers:

[If we do not make the distinction] (1) We might think that, provided you did the right thing, it did not matter how or why you did it – whether you did it willingly or unwillingly, sulkily or cheerfully, through fear of public opinion or for its own sake. But the truth is that right actions done for the wrong reason do not help to build the internal quality or character called a 'virtue', and it is this quality or character that really matters. (If a bad tennis player hits very hard, not because he sees that a very hard stroke is required, but because he has lost his temper, his stroke might possibly, by luck, help him to win that particular game; but it will not be helping him become a reliable player.)

(2) We might think that God wanted simply obedience to a set of rules: whereas He really wants people of a particular sort.[20]

God's will is that acts of ministry be done, but done from the proper heart. How, then, can we pursue true righteousness and avoid doing useless works? I want to answer that by examining how people came up with the idea that righteousness is achieved through works in the first place. For that we will return to the Exodus story.

The Purpose of the Law

After leaving Rephidim, where they had defeated the Amalekites, the Israelites entered the Desert of Sinai and camped in front of the mountain of the same name (Exodus 19:2). There God gave the people the rules, otherwise known as the Law of Moses. The law consists of 613 distinct directives, summarized by the Ten Commandments:

You shall have no other gods before me.

You shall not make for yourself an idol in the form of anything in heaven above or on the earth beneath or in the waters below. You shall not bow down to them or worship them; for I, the LORD your God, am a jealous God, punishing the children for the sin of the fathers to the third and fourth generation of those who hate me, but showing love to a thousand {generations} of those who love me and keep my commandments.

You shall not misuse the name of the LORD your God, for the LORD will not hold anyone guiltless who misuses his name.

Remember the Sabbath day by keeping it holy. Six days you shall labor and do all your work, but the seventh day is a Sabbath to the LORD your God. On it you shall not do any work, neither you, nor your son or daughter, nor your manservant or maidservant, nor your animals, nor the alien within your gates. For in six days the LORD made the heavens and the earth, the sea, and all that is in them, but he rested on the seventh day. Therefore the LORD blessed the Sabbath day and made it holy.

Honor your father and your mother, so that you may live long in the land the LORD your God is giving you.

You shall not murder.

You shall not commit adultery.

You shall not steal.

You shall not give false testimony against your neighbor.

You shall not covet your neighbor's house. You shall not covet your neighbor's wife, or his manservant or maidservant, his ox or donkey, or anything that belongs to your neighbor. (Exodus 20:2-17)

There are obviously many things we could say about the commandments, but for the purpose of our discussion I want to focus on one question: is this list of do's and don'ts primarily an end in itself or is it primarily a means to another end? By that I mean, are the rules ultimately intended as quantifiable expressions of righteousness, or are they meant to help us toward righteousness? Is keeping a commandment inherently righteous, or can a commandment be kept in an unrighteous manner? I am going to argue for the latter in all cases. While the rules certainly have inherent goodness - keeping them is, in and of itself, better than not keeping them, for many practical reasons (the law against murder keeps people safe, for example) - their primary function is character formation.

The temptation when dealing with the commandments is to use them as a checklist for measuring holiness. For example, I could put the Ten Commandments up on my wall and read it every night to evaluate how I've done that day. Did I murder anyone today? Nope. Check. Did I steal anything? Nope. Check. Did I have sex with anyone who wasn't my wife? Nope. Check. Did I make or worship any statues? Nope. Check. And on down the line. As long as I can check off everything (or at least most things) on the list of commands, I must be pretty righteous, right?

Well, no. As we will see, God does not consider you righteous just because you didn't kill anyone today. This is a misunderstanding of the law. Unfortunately, this legalistic approach to the rules has been popular ever since God handed them down. Jesus addressed this mindset in much of his teaching, including his most famous discourse, the Sermon on the Mount.

The Sermon on the Mount

Just as God gave the people the rules from a mountain, Jesus climbed up on one to explain those rules more clearly (Matthew 5:1, 17-20). He started with the sixth commandment:

> You have heard that it was said to the people long ago, "Do not murder, and anyone who murders will be subject to judgment." But I tell you that anyone who is angry with his brother will be subject to judgment. Again, anyone who says to his brother, "Raca," is answerable to the Sanhedrin. But anyone who says, "You fool!" will be in danger of the fire of hell. (Matthew 5:21-22)

Not only are we not to kill one another, Jesus says, but we are not even supposed to get angry with each other. We can't go to the rule list at the end of the day and check off number 6 and think we are doing all right. Instead of asking, "Did I kill anyone today?" we have to ask, "What was my attitude toward other people today?" This gets to the heart of the issue. God doesn't just want to keep you from murdering someone; he wants you to be a forgiving, loving person. God desires a heart condition that is not quantifiable. The rule about murder is to be followed, yes, but it is not the end of the issue. Rather, it is a means to a further end. That end is a pure heart.

My wife and I have a list of rules for our children. For example, they are not allowed to hit each other, they have to wash their hands before meals, and they must say "please" and "thank you" at the appropriate times. We have several reasons for these rules, including our desire to keep them safe from harm and diseases. However, one reason we do not have is the desire for them to grow up and be proud of how polite or clean they are. These rules are not to be used as indicators of righteousness.

We don't want our daughter to grow up and think to herself (or say to anyone else), "I am such a cultured person. Look at how polite and well groomed I am. Why, I don't even hit other people." In fact, that is just the opposite of what we want. These rules are in place to keep the kids humble, not to make them proud. We want them to say "please" as a sign of gratitude and "thank you" as a sign of respect. The rule is designed to point their attention away from themselves and towards the person they are addressing. In the same way, we have a rule about praying before meals. It is intended to generate and keep an attitude of thankfulness to God as we acknowledge our dependence on him. If the prayers turn into displays of self-aggrandizement ("Look at how many flowery words I can say," etc), the rule is being misused.

While we strictly enforce the rule about not hitting, it is not a license for the kids to pinch ("But I didn't *hit* her!"). We want the interpersonal relationship rules to guide the children toward actually caring about the well-being of their siblings. In the same way, personal hygiene rules are intended to engender a respect for one's body and a desire for healthy living. The heart condition is what is ultimately important; the rules are primarily a means to that end.

This is what Jesus explained as he continued through his sermon to the next example. The Old Testament law was given to the world for the same reason that rules are given to children: to lead them toward righteousness of the heart.

The rules are to be kept, but are not to be understood as the end-all and be-all of righteousness.

"You have heard that it was said, 'Do not commit adultery.' But I tell you that anyone who looks at a woman lustfully has already committed adultery with her in his heart" (Matthew 5:27-28). Jesus says that it is not enough just to not have sex with someone who is not your spouse. You are not even to lust. You are to be a faithful person in your heart. You are use the law to develop a character quality, not treat it as a task to be check marked.

> Again, you have heard that it was said to the people long ago, "Do not break your oath, but keep the oaths you have made to the Lord." But I tell you, Do not swear at all: either by heaven, for it is God's throne; or by the earth, for it is his footstool; or by Jerusalem, for it is the city of the Great King. And do not swear by your head, for you cannot make even one hair white or black. Simply let your "Yes" be "Yes," and your "No," "No"; anything beyond this comes from the evil one. (Matthew 5:33-37)

The religious leaders of Jesus' time had developed a system of rules to elaborate on the injunction to "keep your oaths." The list explained when a person had to keep their word and when it was OK not to. If one swore "by the earth" it meant one thing, and if the same person swore "by Jerusalem" it meant another, for example. It was a bit like the rules that grade school students use to test credibility: to "pinky swear" means a vow must be kept, but if fingers were crossed at the time of the promise, it doesn't need to be kept.

Jesus cuts through that nonsense by saying that we are simply to be trustworthy people. Keeping our word is not a matter of doing what the law says; it is about being a certain type of person. Jesus implies that if we have to use an oath to back up our promise, there is a problem already. If we tell someone we are going to do something and then have to follow that up with "I swear," it is probably an indication that we have let that person down in the past and are not entirely trustworthy.

> You have heard that it was said, "Eye for eye, and tooth for tooth." But I tell you, Do not resist an evil person. If someone strikes you on the right cheek, turn to him the other also. And if someone wants to sue you and take your tunic, let him have your cloak as well. If someone forces you to go one mile, go with him two miles. Give to the one who asks you, and do not turn away from the one who wants to borrow from you.

> You have heard that it was said, "Love your neighbor and hate your enemy." But I tell you: Love your enemies and pray for those who persecute you, that you may be sons of your Father in heaven. He causes his sun to rise on the evil and the good, and sends rain on the righteous and the unrighteous. If you love those who love you, what reward will you get? Are not even the tax collectors doing that? And if you greet only your brothers, what are you doing more than others? Do not even pagans do that? Be perfect, therefore, as your heavenly Father is perfect. (Matthew 5:38-48)

The background for this part of the sermon is the idea that justice should be proportionate. The rules stated that if someone harmed another person, they were due that amount of harm in return and not more, while those that treated people well were due that friendship in return. The goal was to keep acts of vengeance from escalating out of control. The idea was to keep people from killing each other over name-calling, for example. An eye for an eye was enough, an eye and a leg for an eye was too much. Justice was encouraged, disproportionate vengeance was not. However, Jesus says even avoiding vengeance is not enough. The rule was meant to push people to an even higher standard. We are to be the kind of people who actually love our enemies and seek their good. In short, we should be perfect. This is God's will.

Jesus then moved into the realm of what some would consider religious observances, but what should rightly be called spiritual disciplines. He talked about tithing, prayer and fasting.

> Be careful not to do your "acts of righteousness" before men, to be seen by them. If you do, you will have no reward from your Father in heaven.
>
> So when you give to the needy, do not announce it with trumpets, as the hypocrites do in the synagogues and on the streets, to be honored by men. I tell you the truth, they have received their reward in full. But when you give to the needy, do not let your left hand know what your right hand is doing, so that your giving may be in secret. Then your Father, who sees what is done in secret, will reward you.
>
> And when you pray, do not be like the hypocrites, for they love to pray standing in the synagogues and on the street corners to be seen by men. I tell you the truth, they have received their reward in full. But when you pray, go into your room, close the door and pray to your Father, who is unseen. Then your Father, who sees what is done in secret, will reward you. And when you pray, do not keep on babbling like pagans, for they think they will be heard because of their many words. Do not be like them, for your Father knows what you need before you ask him.

This, then, is how you should pray: "Our Father in heaven, hallowed be your name, your kingdom come, your will be done on earth as it is in heaven. Give us today our daily bread. Forgive us our debts, as we also have forgiven our debtors. And lead us not into temptation, but deliver us from the evil one."

For if you forgive men when they sin against you, your heavenly Father will also forgive you. But if you do not forgive men their sins, your Father will not forgive your sins.

When you fast, do not look somber as the hypocrites do, for they disfigure their faces to show men they are fasting. I tell you the truth, they have received their reward in full. But when you fast, put oil on your head and wash your face, so that it will not be obvious to men that you are fasting, but only to your Father, who is unseen; and your Father, who sees what is done in secret, will reward you. (Matthew 6:1-18)

As I already talked about regarding my children's prayers, spiritual disciplines are not to be done for show. They are to make you humble and draw you closer to God, not make you proud and send you farther away from him. Again and again Jesus scolded the Pharisees for this misuse of the law.

Then Jesus said to the crowds and to his disciples: "The teachers of the law and the Pharisees sit in Moses' seat. So you must obey them and do everything they tell you. But do not do what they do, for they do not practice what they preach. They tie up heavy loads and put them on men's shoulders, but they themselves are not willing to lift a finger to move them.

"Everything they do is done for men to see: They make their phylacteries wide and the tassels on their garments long; they love the place of honor at banquets and the most important seats in the synagogues; they love to be greeted in the marketplaces and to have men call them 'Rabbi.'

"But you are not to be called 'Rabbi,' for you have only one Master and you are all brothers. And do not call anyone on earth 'father,' for you have one Father, and he is in heaven. Nor are you to be called 'teacher,' for you have one Teacher, the Christ. The greatest among you will be your servant. For whoever exalts himself will be humbled, and whoever humbles himself will be exalted.

"Woe to you, teachers of the law and Pharisees, you hypocrites! You shut the kingdom of heaven in men's faces. You yourselves do not enter, nor will you let those enter who are trying to.

"Woe to you, teachers of the law and Pharisees, you hypocrites! You travel over land and sea to win a single convert, and when he becomes one, you make him twice as much a son of hell as you are.

"Woe to you, blind guides! You say, 'If anyone swears by the temple, it means nothing; but if anyone swears by the gold of the temple, he is bound by his oath.' You blind fools! Which is greater: the gold, or the temple that makes the gold sacred? You also say, 'If anyone swears by the altar, it means nothing; but if anyone swears by the gift on it, he is bound by his oath.' You blind men! Which is greater: the gift, or the altar that makes the gift sacred? Therefore, he who swears by the altar swears by it and by everything on it. And he who swears by the temple swears by it and by the one who dwells in it. And he who swears by heaven swears by God's throne and by the one who sits on it.

"Woe to you, teachers of the law and Pharisees, you hypocrites! You give a tenth of your spices – mint, dill and cummin. But you have neglected the more important matters of the law – justice, mercy and faithfulness. You should have practiced the latter, without neglecting the former. You blind guides! You strain out a gnat but swallow a camel.

"Woe to you, teachers of the law and Pharisees, you hypocrites! You clean the outside of the cup and dish, but inside they are full of greed and self-indulgence. Blind Pharisee! First clean the inside of the cup and dish, and then the outside also will be clean.

"Woe to you, teachers of the law and Pharisees, you hypocrites! You are like whitewashed tombs, which look beautiful on the outside but on the inside are full of dead men's bones and everything unclean. In the same way, on the outside you appear to people as righteous but on the inside you are full of hypocrisy and wickedness." (Mathew 23:1-28)

It doesn't get any clearer than that. Righteousness is not keeping the letter of the law in an outward show of obedience; it is a heart condition. Righteousness is qualitative, not quantitative. The Pharisees were very good at checking items off their daily list of rules and duties, but they missed the point. Notice that Jesus tells them they have "neglected the more important matter of the law – justice, mercy and faithfulness." This is just what we have been saying. God wants us to be a certain type of person: one that is just and merciful and faithful. As God explains in Hosea 6:6, "I desire mercy not sacrifice, acknowledgment of God rather than burnt offerings" God does not need a percentage of our possessions as if that offering was good in and of itself. He desires that we be righteous on the inside.

Applying This Principle to Acts of Service

This principle applies not only to the keeping of the law and to spiritual disciplines, but to all of our acts of service. This is where we started at the beginning of the chapter. Why does God approve of some people's ministry and not others? Because some acts flow from a righteous heart, while others do not. The miracle workers who show up on judgment day and are condemned (Matthew 7:21-23) have obviously been viewing the religious acts as righteous in and of themselves. This is a great example of the works that Paul tells us are useless at procuring salvation (Ephesians 2:8-9). God does not want us to do ministry simply for the sake of doing ministry. It must flow from an inner righteousness.

Paul explains that even the greatest acts of ministry in the world are pointless if they are not done by a loving person:

> If I speak in the tongues of men and of angels, but have not love, I am only a resounding gong or a clanging cymbal. If I have the gift of prophecy and can fathom all mysteries and all knowledge, and if I have a faith that can move mountains, but have not love, I am nothing. If I give all I possess to the poor and surrender my body to the flames, but have not love, I gain nothing.

Love is patient, love is kind. It does not envy, it does not boast, it is not proud. It is not rude, it is not self-seeking, it is not easily angered, it keeps no record of wrongs. Love does not delight in evil but rejoices with the truth. It always protects, always trusts, always hopes, always perseveres. (1 Corinthians 13:1-7)

It is easy to get into the habit of quantifying our spiritual life. We judge our righteousness by how many activities we can cram into our busy schedule. Look back at the list of actions we made at the beginning of this chapter. Do you see them as duties to be checked off a list each week or do they flow from your heart?

I visited a church once that had every congregant's name on a list in the foyer. Beside each name was a row of boxes to check, each representing an activity that the people were to have taken part in the previous week. Did you read your Bible twice a day? Check. Did you evangelize at least five people this week? Check. Did you give your offering? Check. Was this supposed to indicate righteousness?

While we may not all be so public about quantifying our virtue, we often do the same thing more subtly. We forget that the Christian enterprise is about making people holy, not keeping them busy.

I remember visiting a different church with a traveling ministry team. We pulled up in front of the building and jumped out of our van to unload equipment and ask for specific directions. Before we could do any of that, though, the senior pastor came out and screamed at us for parking where we weren't supposed to. I couldn't believe what a jerk the guy was. That pastor had the biggest church in town, with programs that ran like well-oiled machines. He had all the outward trappings of successful religion but (at least on that day) he neglected the more important matter of inner righteousness displayed in mercy and patience. He did not love us.

Judgment Day

We don't want to show up on judgment day saying, "Look at all we did" like the people in the "Lord, Lord" passage of Matthew 7. Instead we should hope to stand before God like the people Jesus talks about in Matthew 25.

> When the Son of Man comes in his glory, and all the angels with him, he will sit on his throne in heavenly glory. All the nations will be gathered before him, and he will separate the people one from another as a shepherd separates the sheep from the goats. He will put the sheep on his right and the goats on his left.

> Then the King will say to those on his right, "Come, you who are blessed by my Father; take your inheritance, the kingdom prepared for you since the creation of the world. For I was hungry and you gave me something to eat, I was thirsty and you gave me something to drink, I was a stranger and you invited me in, I needed clothes and you clothed me, I was sick and you looked after me, I was in prison and you came to visit me."

> Then the righteous will answer him, "Lord, when did we see you hungry and feed you, or thirsty and give you something to drink? When did we see you a stranger and invite you in, or needing clothes and clothe you? When did we see you sick or in prison and go to visit you?"

> The King will reply, "I tell you the truth, whatever you did for one of the least of these brothers of mine, you did for me." (Matt 25:31-40)

Notice that the people who make it into Heaven in this passage had also been busy working. However, the difference between these folks and the "evildoers" of Matthew 7 is the servants in Matthew 25 didn't focus on the deeds as an end in themselves. Indeed, they didn't focus on them at all – they couldn't even remember doing them. This shows that they were just the type of people who helped others in need. They were loving, kind, generous and humble. They weren't looking at their works with pride or as a reason for their righteousness. These are the kind of people Jesus welcomes into the Promised Land. These people have the character traits he is looking for. On the other hand, if they had shown up and said, "Look at how we worked in the homeless shelter, Lord," they would have been rejected for having the wrong approach to service.

Conclusion

We are not to obey the rules as an end in themselves but because they are a means toward helping us become righteous people. God handed down the commandments to help develop character, not as the benchmark of character. The mark of a disciple is not busyness, but holiness. True righteousness is the goal of redemption. Developing character is an absolutely essential part of our journey. As Peter argues, we must continue to become more and more like Jesus.

> His divine power has given us everything we need for life and godliness through our knowledge of him who called us by his own glory and goodness. Through these he has given us his very great and precious promises, so that through them you may participate in the divine nature and escape the corruption in the world caused by evil desires.

For this very reason, make every effort to add to your faith goodness; and to goodness, knowledge; and to knowledge, self-control; and to self-control, perseverance; and to perseverance, godliness; and to godliness, brotherly kindness; and to brotherly kindness, love. For if you possess these qualities in increasing measure, they will keep you from being ineffective and unproductive in your knowledge of our Lord Jesus Christ. But if anyone does not have them, he is nearsighted and blind, and has forgotten that he has been cleansed from his past sins. (2 Peter 1:3-9)

CHAPTER 9

The Seriousness of Sin

The LORD replied to Moses, "Whoever has sinned against me I will blot out of my book. Now go, lead the people to the place I spoke of, and my angel will go before you. However, when the time comes for me to punish, I will punish them for their sin." And the LORD struck the people with a plague because of what they did with the calf Aaron had made.

EXODUS 32:33-35

For the wages of sin is death, but the gift of God is eternal life in Christ Jesus our Lord.

ROMANS 6:23

Sin is No Big Deal, Right?

I spent the last chapter trying to convince you that the main point of the law is character development, and I concluded by saying that holiness is an "essential part of our journey."

I'm going to take the next two chapters to emphasize the word *essential*. I often get the impression that people think developing holiness is like living the "Eddie Bauer"[21] edition of the Christian life. It's nice and all, but you don't *really* need it. These people have the idea that actually becoming like Jesus is OK for really fanatical people, but for the vast majority, a more moderate approach is just fine. This attitude is revealed in sentiments like, "It is so great that God is a God of grace and that it doesn't really matter what kind of lives we live. So I gossip a little here or cut a few ethical corners there, God still loves me." You see it in statements such as, "I know that what I am doing is wrong, but we are about grace here, not judgment," and even in the bumper sticker slogan, "I'm not perfect, just forgiven."

These sayings are promoting the idea, one that has become pervasive in many churches, that sin is simply not that big of a deal. The underlying assumption is that it does not matter if you sin because sin has no *ultimate* significance. Sin does not keep you from having a relationship with God, and it certainly doesn't keep you from getting to Heaven, so why worry about it? If righteousness fanatics and mediocre sinners all end up in the same place anyway, there is simply not much motivation to diligently pursue righteousness. In fact, diligently pursuing holiness is sometimes scorned within this framework. The "regular folk" look down on those who are not content to live in ethical mediocrity as "overly zealous," like the people who not only get the Eddie Bauer package, but then outfit their new SUV with 24 karat gold wheels. Can't you hear the whispering? "Now that's just ostentatious. Can't those people stop showing off and just be plain like the rest of us? I am so glad that I can be content with who I am."

I think the idea that sin has no really severe consequences is a major reason that so many polls reveal the morality of Christians to be essentially the same as the morality of non-

Christians.[22] For example, studies have found that some 40% of pastors consume porn on a regular basis.[23] Speaking of evangelicals in particular, but making a statement that is applicable across the Christian spectrum, Michael Horton laments: "Christians are as likely to embrace lifestyles every bit as hedonistic, materialistic, self-centered, and sexually immoral as the world in general."[24]

Is this a big deal? Is sin serious? Where does holiness come into the plan of salvation? Is it necessary? Does everyone end up in the same place regardless of their moral quality?

Let's start answering these questions by looking at how Peter finished the train of thought he started in the passage with which we concluded Chapter 8. He explained that we should be adding righteous character qualities to our lives and then ended by pointing out the important ramifications of continuing to become holy: "Therefore, my brothers, be all the more eager to make your calling and election sure. For if you do these things, you will never fall, and you will receive a rich welcome into the eternal kingdom of our Lord and Savior Jesus Christ" (2 Peter 1:10-11).

According to Peter, as long as you are growing in righteousness, you will never fall and will receive a rich welcome into Heaven. But what is the implication if you are not becoming like Jesus? A plain-sense reading of the text suggests that those who do not grow in righteousness are in danger of falling and not receiving a rich welcome in the eternal Kingdom. I believe that is correct. In explaining the benefits of growing in righteousness, Peter is also issuing a warning about the peril of not growing in righteousness. In this chapter I will expand on this warning and argue that the reason growing in righteousness is so important is that sin, *at any stage in your journey to the Promised Land*, causes a rift in your relationship with God and puts you in danger of not making it into Heaven. Only those who persevere in their relationship with God and thereby grow in holiness all the way to the end of the expedition get in. Holiness is not an "add-on" to the Christian life. It is not the leather seats or gold wheels, which are nice but unessential. Rather, righteousness is the essential standard equipment. It is the chassis and the engine. You can't get across the wilderness without it.

Warnings from the Exodus Story

As it has throughout our study, the Exodus story provides us with our primary illustration of this truth. Many Israelites started out on the journey to the Promised Land, but very few actually finished and made it in. Even though these Hebrews escaped Egypt, passed through the Red Sea and experienced God's miraculous provision in the desert, sin brought them down. As Paul clearly explains, this is an illustration of what can happen to Christians who allow sin to keep them from finishing the journey. After calling on his readers to run the race to the end and fight the war in such a way as to win rather than to lose, he explains why:

> For I do not want you to be ignorant of the fact, brothers, that our forefathers were all under the cloud and that they all passed through the sea. They were all baptized into Moses in the cloud and in the sea. They all ate the same spiritual food and drank the same spiritual drink; for they drank from the spiritual rock that accompanied them, and that rock was Christ. Nevertheless, God was not pleased with most of them; their bodies were scattered over the desert.

> Now these things occurred as examples to keep us from setting our hearts on evil things as they did. Do not be idolaters, as some of them were; as it is written: "The people sat down to eat and drink and got up to indulge in pagan revelry." We should not commit

sexual immorality, as some of them did – and in one day twenty-three thousand of them died. We should not test the Lord, as some of them did – and were killed by snakes. And do not grumble, as some of them did – and were killed by the destroying angel.

These things happened to them as examples and were written down as warnings for us, on whom the fulfillment of the ages has come. So, if you think you are standing firm, be careful that you don't fall! (1 Corinthians 10:1-12)

The importance of the Exodus story in understanding the gospel of Jesus doesn't get any clearer than that! Paul says that the Israelite's journey through the Red Sea was symbolic of the baptism that a Christian undergoes at the beginning of his or her journey. This is just what we have been saying. To get to the Promised Land, the Israelites had to be freed from the power of Pharaoh and the penalty of God's judgment and walk out of Egypt under the blood of the lamb. To get to Heaven we need to be freed from Satan's power and the penalty of God's judgment by getting under the blood of our lamb, Jesus. We then are baptized[25] and begin the next stage of the journey home, just as the Israelites were baptized in the Red Sea as they began a new stage in their journey. After making these connections, Paul explicitly states that we are to learn from the Israelites' example so that we don't repeat their mistake and "fall." Paul doesn't want us to end up dead in the wilderness rather than home in the Promised Land.

So what exactly did the Israelites do? Paul references several events, beginning with perhaps the most severe. "The people sat down to eat and drink and got up to indulge in pagan revelry" is a quote from Exodus 32, a chapter explaining what happened as the people were waiting for

Moses to come down from Mount Sinai. We will start with that episode as well.

The Golden Calf

> When the people saw that Moses was so long in coming down from the mountain, they gathered around Aaron and said, "Come, make us gods who will go before us. As for this fellow Moses who brought us up out of Egypt, we don't know what has happened to him."

> Aaron answered them, "Take off the gold earrings that your wives, your sons and your daughters are wearing, and bring them to me." So all the people took off their earrings and brought them to Aaron. He took what they handed him and made it into an idol cast in the shape of a calf, fashioning it with a tool. Then they said, "These are your gods, O Israel, who brought you up out of Egypt."

> When Aaron saw this, he built an altar in front of the calf and announced, "Tomorrow there will be a festival to the LORD." So the next day the people rose early and sacrificed burnt offerings and presented fellowship offerings. Afterward they sat down to eat and drink and got up to indulge in revelry.

> Then the LORD said to Moses, "Go down, because your people, whom you brought up out of Egypt, have become corrupt. They have been quick to turn away from what I commanded them and have made themselves an idol cast in the shape of a calf. They have bowed down to it and sacrificed to it and have

said, 'These are your gods, O Israel, who brought
you up out of Egypt.'

"I have seen these people," the LORD said to Moses,
"and they are a stiff-necked people. Now leave me
alone so that my anger may burn against them and
that I may destroy them. Then I will make you into a
great nation."

But Moses sought the favor of the LORD his God.
"O LORD," he said, "why should your anger burn
against your people, whom you brought out of Egypt
with great power and a mighty hand? Why should the
Egyptians say, 'It was with evil intent that he brought
them out, to kill them in the mountains and to wipe
them off the face of the earth'? Turn from your fierce
anger; relent and do not bring disaster on your people.
Remember your servants Abraham, Isaac and Israel, to
whom you swore by your own self: 'I will make your
descendants as numerous as the stars in the sky and
I will give your descendants all this land I promised
them, and it will be their inheritance forever.'" Then
the LORD relented and did not bring on his people the
disaster he had threatened.

Moses turned and went down the mountain with the
two tablets of the Testimony in his hands. They were
inscribed on both sides, front and back. The tablets
were the work of God; the writing was the writing of
God, engraved on the tablets.

When Joshua heard the noise of the people shouting,
he said to Moses, "There is the sound of war in the
camp."

Moses replied: "It is not the sound of victory, it is not the sound of defeat; it is the sound of singing that I hear."

When Moses approached the camp and saw the calf and the dancing, his anger burned and he threw the tablets out of his hands, breaking them to pieces at the foot of the mountain. And he took the calf they had made and burned it in the fire; then he ground it to powder, scattered it on the water and made the Israelites drink it.

He said to Aaron, "What did these people do to you, that you led them into such great sin?"

"Do not be angry, my lord," Aaron answered. "You know how prone these people are to evil. They said to me, 'Make us gods who will go before us. As for this fellow Moses who brought us up out of Egypt, we don't know what has happened to him.' So I told them, 'Whoever has any gold jewelry, take it off.' Then they gave me the gold, and I threw it into the fire, and out came this calf!"

Moses saw that the people were running wild and that Aaron had let them get out of control and so become a laughingstock to their enemies. So he stood at the entrance to the camp and said, "Whoever is for the LORD, come to me." And all the Levites rallied to him.

Then he said to them, "This is what the LORD, the God of Israel, says: 'Each man strap a sword to his side. Go back and forth through the camp from one end to the other, each killing his brother and friend and neighbor.'" The Levites did as Moses commanded, and that day about three thousand of the people died. Then Moses said, "You have been set apart to the LORD today, for you were against your own sons and brothers, and he has blessed you this day."

The next day Moses said to the people, "You have committed a great sin. But now I will go up to the LORD; perhaps I can make atonement for your sin."

So Moses went back to the LORD and said, "Oh, what a great sin these people have committed! They have made themselves gods of gold. But now, please forgive their sin—but if not, then blot me out of the book you have written."

The LORD replied to Moses, "Whoever has sinned against me I will blot out of my book. Now go, lead the people to the place I spoke of, and my angel will go before you. However, when the time comes for me to punish, I will punish them for their sin."

And the LORD struck the people with a plague because of what they did with the calf Aaron had made. (Exodus 32:1-35)

The people succumbed to idolatry and God blotted them out of his book. They made it out of Egypt, but they died in the desert due to sin. Why was God so harsh? The bottom line is that sin leads to death. Always.

Sin Equals Death

Satan's biggest lie is that if we sin we "will not surely die" (Genesis 3:4). He used it on Adam and Eve in the

Garden of Eden and has continued to try it on every person since. As our first parents and the Israelites learned the hard way, Satan is wrong. The truth is, "The wages of sin is death" (Romans 6:23).

Relationships are based on a covenant of trust. Breaking that covenant breaks relationship. Sinning against God breaks relationship with him in the same way that lying to or cheating on one's spouse breaks relationship with him or her. One cannot commit adultery and think that everything is going to remain all right. Trust has been broken and a schism is the result. This is exactly what happens when we sin against God. Adam and Eve were kicked out of the Garden of Eden and the Children of Israel were not allowed to enter the Promised Land. Breaking relationship with God keeps us from his presence and being out of the presence of God is hell. Literally.

Now you might say, "But, Don, look at the rest of Romans 6:23. The wages of sin may be death, but 'the gift of God is eternal life in Christ Jesus our Lord.' Doesn't that mean that our sin is now covered, or at least can be covered, by Jesus?"

This idea is common and often arises in the context of using this text as an evangelistic tool. People quote it to potential converts in explaining that although everyone sins and is deserving of death, God gives Christians the gift of eternal life through Jesus instead.

This is a severe misuse of this text. These teachers are essentially paraphrasing the verse something like this: "The wages of sin for an unbeliever is death, but a Christian can sin without consequence because of Jesus." The only way to reach this understanding is to insert a conditional timeline to the principle that sin equals death: "The wages of sin used to be death for me, but since I came to Jesus I have become exempt from that rule."

These interpretations are completely unwarranted and in fact result in a teaching that is *exactly the opposite* of what

Paul intended. Paul is not telling non-Christians that they can escape the penalty of current sins by turning to Jesus. He is writing to Christians with a warning that they are not to use God's grace as a license to sin because the unchangeable rule of the universe is that sin leads to death! This becomes apparent when you look at the rest of Romans 6.

You No Longer Have to Sin, So Don't

Paul's argument in the first part of Romans 6 can be summarized, "Since Christ has enabled us to live righteous lives we should no longer sin." Again and again Paul rails against sin, explaining that since Christ has set us free, we should no longer live as slaves.

> What shall we say, then? Shall we go on sinning so that grace may increase? By no means! We died to sin; how can we live in it any longer? Or don't you know that all of us who were baptized into Christ Jesus were baptized into his death? We were therefore buried with him through baptism into death in order that, just as Christ was raised from the dead through the glory of the Father, we too may live a new life.
>
> If we have been united with him like this in his death, we will certainly also be united with him in his resurrection. For we know that our old self was crucified with him so that the body of sin might be done away with, that we should no longer be slaves to sin – because anyone who has died has been freed from sin.
>
> Now if we died with Christ, we believe that we will also live with him. For we know that since Christ was raised from the dead, he cannot die again; death no longer has mastery over him. The death he died,

he died to sin once for all; but the life he lives, he lives to God.

In the same way, count yourselves dead to sin but alive to God in Christ Jesus. Therefore do not let sin reign in your mortal body so that you obey its evil desires. Do not offer the parts of your body to sin, as instruments of wickedness, but rather offer yourselves to God, as those who have been brought from death to life; and offer the parts of your body to him as instruments of righteousness. For sin shall not be your master, because you are not under law, but under grace. (Romans 6:1-14)

Paul then adds some serious emphasis to his point by reminding his readers of the consequences of sin. He points out that the penalty for sin is still the same as it always has been: death. Since nobody should want death, especially when life is offered to them through Jesus, they should stop sinning and accept life. As you read the rest of the passage, notice the formula Paul uses in contrasting our two options:

Sin = Separation from God (Death)
Grace (Being Set Free) = Obedience, Righteousness, Holiness = Eternal Life

Sin is always associated directly with death, and God's grace is always associated directly with righteousness, which is linked directly to eternal life.

What then? Shall we sin because we are not under law but under grace? By no means! Don't you know that when you offer yourselves to someone to obey him as slaves, you are slaves to the one whom you obey – whether you are slaves to sin, which leads to death, or to obedience, which leads to righteousness? But thanks be to God that, though you used to be slaves to sin, you wholeheartedly obeyed the form of teaching to which you were entrusted. You have been set free from sin and have become slaves to righteousness.

I put this in human terms because you are weak in your natural selves. Just as you used to offer the parts of your body in slavery to impurity and to ever-increasing wickedness, so now offer them in slavery to righteousness leading to holiness. When you were slaves to sin, you were free from the control of righteousness. What benefit did you reap at that time from the things you are now ashamed of? Those things result in death! But now that you have been set free from sin and have become slaves to God, the benefit you reap leads to holiness, and the result is eternal life. For the wages of sin is death, but the gift of God is eternal life in Christ Jesus our Lord. (Romans 6:15-23)

So Paul's full argument in Romans 6 is that Jesus has set us free from having to sin, which is good because sin leads to death. Because of Jesus' work, we are now able to live righteously, which is also good, because holiness leads to eternal life. Therefore, we should choose life by living holy lives! Don't sin, lest we die!

The fact is, sin leads to death; it separates us from God. This is a hard and fast rule of the universe. It applies to everyone. As Isaiah explained (to believers), "Your iniquities have separated you from your God; your sins have hidden his face from you" (Isaiah 59:2). That is why the writer of Hebrews can say, "Without holiness, *no one* will see the Lord" (Hebrews 12:14, emphasis mine).

It is easy to emphasize the importance of God's forgiveness in salvation, but we must not forget that forgiveness is just the first step in the process. Becoming holy is part of the plan, too. Jesus didn't come just to forgive sin; he came to eradicate it. His goal for us is holiness.

For example, when faced with a woman caught in adultery, Jesus didn't condemn her. However, he didn't tell her that everything was alright, either. Sin was her problem and, he told her to get rid of it.

> Jesus bent down and started to write on the ground with his finger. When [the religious leaders who had brought the woman before Jesus] kept on questioning him, he straightened up and said to them, "If any one of you is without sin, let him be the first to throw a stone at her." Again he stooped down and wrote on the ground.
>
> At this, those who heard began to go away one at a time, the older ones first, until only Jesus was left, with the woman still standing there. Jesus straightened up and asked her, "Woman, where are they? Has no one condemned you?"
>
> "No one, sir," she said.
>
> "Then neither do I condemn you," Jesus declared. "Go now and leave your life of sin." (John 8:7-11)

Jesus had a similar message for the man he healed at the pool of Bethesda. Jesus said to him, "See, you are well again. Stop sinning or something worse may happen to you" (John 5:14).

Jesus saw the danger of sin so clearly that he even recommended, hyperbolically, self-mutilation as a reasonable alternative. After all, it is better to lose a hand than be sent to hell.

You have heard that it was said, "Do not commit adultery." But I tell you that anyone who looks at a woman lustfully has already committed adultery with her in his heart. If your right eye causes you to sin, gouge it out and throw it away. It is better for you to lose one part of your body than for your whole body to be thrown into hell. And if your right hand causes you to sin, cut it off and throw it away. It is better for you to lose one part of your body than for your whole body to go into hell. (Matthew 5:27-30)

Here, Jesus clearly equated sinning with entering Hell. If Hell is defined as separation from God, and sin separates, then Jesus was making the point of this chapter exactly.

Jesus' forgiveness is always accompanied by a call to holiness. It is one thing to make it through Passover, to be covered by the blood of the lamb and escape punishment. It is quite another thing to make it across the wilderness. The wilderness is the spiritual formation part of the journey, where we are made into the type of person God wants us to be. The two segments of the journey can never be separated. Eternal life cannot be obtained by stopping at Passover or the Red Sea or Mount Sinai. We must not stop at being forgiven by Jesus. We must also become holy.

Depending on your theological background, you now might be thinking, "But what about the most famous verse in the Bible? What about John 3:16: 'For God so loved the world that he gave his one and only Son, that whoever believes in him shall not perish but have eternal life.'? There doesn't seem to be anything about holiness in there."

There is, actually, if you look at the context. This verse is in a passage in which Jesus explains to Nicodemus what is required for eternal life. Jesus tells Nicodemus that he must be born again (John 3:3). By this Jesus meant that Nicodemus had to become a completely new person, one who was born of the spirit rather than flesh (John 3:5-7). We will talk more about what this means in Chapter 11, but for now I want to emphasize that this new person is characterized by ever-increasing holiness.

God explained through Ezekiel that he would create new people by giving them a new spirit, *so that humans could be righteous.* "I will give them an undivided heart and put a new spirit in them; I will remove from them their heart of stone and give them a heart of flesh" (Ezekiel 11:19, also echoed in Ezekiel 36:26).

God's intent is that we be holy. There is no contingency in his mission for this not to take place. There is no backup route to the Promised Land for those who do not become righteous. The Nicodemus passage concludes with stark moral language contrasting those who get eternal life with those who don't. Those who hang on to their evil deeds are left in the darkness.

> This is the verdict: Light has come into the world, but men loved darkness instead of light because their deeds were evil. Everyone who does evil hates the light, and will not come into the light for fear that his deeds will be exposed. But whoever lives by the truth comes into the light, so that it may be seen plainly that what he has done has been done through God. (John 3:19-21)

Is righteousness important? Yes! Is sin a big deal? Yes! These verses from John 3 state the exact formula we talked about from Romans 6. They simply add some more descriptive terminology to it.

> Sin (Living According to Flesh) = Separation from God (Death)

Grace (Being Born Again, Living According to the Spirit) = Holiness = Eternal Life

The fact that living by the Spirit is characterized by holiness is a strong New Testament theme. For instance, Paul contrasts life in the flesh and life in the spirit by focusing on the different moral characteristics of each.

So I say, live by the Spirit, and you will not gratify the desires of the sinful nature. For the sinful nature desires what is contrary to the Spirit, and the Spirit what is contrary to the sinful nature. They are in conflict with each other, so that you do not do what you want. But if you are led by the Spirit, you are not under law.

The acts of the sinful nature are obvious: sexual immorality, impurity and debauchery; idolatry and witchcraft; hatred, discord, jealousy, fits of rage, selfish ambition, dissensions, factions and envy; drunkenness, orgies, and the like. I warn you, as I did before, that those who live like this will not inherit the kingdom of God.

But the fruit of the Spirit is love, joy, peace, patience, kindness, goodness, faithfulness, gentleness and self-control. Against such things there is no law. Those who belong to Christ Jesus have crucified the sinful nature with its passions and desires. (Galatians 5:16-24)

The mark of a true follower of Christ, one who is living by the Spirit, is holiness. On the other hand, a life lived apart from the Spirit is easily discernible by its unrighteousness. Notice the strong language of Ephesians 5. Paul makes a point of declaring that immoral people do not get into the

Kingdom, and for this reason we should strive to live righteously by the Spirit.

> Be imitators of God, therefore, as dearly loved children and live a life of love, just as Christ loved us and gave himself up for us as a fragrant offering and sacrifice to God.

> But among you there must not be even a hint of sexual immorality, or of any kind of impurity, or of greed, because these are improper for God's holy people. Nor should there be obscenity, foolish talk or coarse joking, which are out of place, but rather thanksgiving. For of this you can be sure: No immoral, impure or greedy person – such a man is an idolater – has any inheritance in the kingdom of Christ and of God Let no one deceive you with empty words, for because of such things God's wrath comes on those who are disobedient. Therefore do not be partners with them.

> For you were once darkness, but now you are light in the Lord. Live as children of light (for the fruit of the light consists in all goodness, righteousness and truth) and find out what pleases the Lord. Have nothing to do with the fruitless deeds of darkness, but rather expose them. For it is shameful even to mention what the disobedient do in secret. But everything exposed by the light becomes visible, for it is light that makes everything visible. This is why it is said: "Wake up, O sleeper, rise from the dead, and Christ will shine on you."

> Be very careful, then, how you live – not as unwise but as wise, making the most of every opportunity, because

the days are evil. Therefore do not be foolish, but understand what the Lord's will is. Do not get drunk on wine, which leads to debauchery. Instead, be filled with the Spirit. (Ephesians 5:1-18)

In the second to last chapter in the Bible, Jesus explains who will inherit eternal life and who will not. Notice the categories he uses. Those who overcome get the Kingdom while the wicked are sent to Hell. Jesus again makes plain that righteousness is imperative, and sin cannot be tolerated.

> [Jesus] said to me: "It is done. I am the Alpha and the Omega, the Beginning and the End. To him who is thirsty I will give to drink without cost from the spring of the water of life. He who overcomes will inherit all this, and I will be his God and he will be my son. But the cowardly, the unbelieving, the vile, the murderers, the sexually immoral, those who practice magic arts, the idolaters and all liars – their place will be in the fiery lake of burning sulfur. This is the second death." (Revelation 21:6-8)

"But Nobody's Perfect"

Before moving on, I want to address one more possible objection to the argument presented in this chapter. You might be thinking something like this: "But Don, this picture is too bleak. Nobody's perfect. We all sin. According to your logic, we are all going to end up in Hell."

Well, hopefully not. It is certainly true that everyone sins. It is also true that some of these sinners will go to Heaven. The key to reconciling this apparent contradiction is to remember that broken relationships can be restored through confession and forgiveness. While sin separates us from God, repentant confession of that sin combined with God's forgiveness enables that relationship to continue growing.

The Apostle John describes how this works in his first epistle. In the passage below, he starts by affirming the point we have been making about the necessity of righteousness.

> This is the message we have heard from him and declare to you: God is light; in him there is no darkness at all. If we claim to have fellowship with him yet walk in the darkness, we lie and do not live by the truth. But if we walk in the light, as he is in the light, we have fellowship with one another, and the blood of Jesus, his Son, purifies us from all sin. (1 John 1:5-7)

John says that true believers walk in the light and are purified from sin. Those who continue their life of unrighteousness do not live in the light or by the truth. Basically, John argues that Christians should be living holy lives. However, he realizes that nobody is perfect and anticipates the objection we have raised, so he explains what to do when we fall short: confess our sins.

> If we claim to be without sin, we deceive ourselves and the truth is not in us. If we confess our sins, he is faithful and just and will forgive us our sins and purify us from all unrighteousness. If we claim we have not sinned, we make him out to be a liar and his word has no place in our lives.

> My dear children, I write this to you so that you will not sin. But if anybody does sin, we have one who speaks to the Father in our defense – Jesus Christ, the Righteous One. He is the atoning sacrifice for our sins, and not only for ours but also for the sins of the whole world. (1 John 1:8-2:2).

John tells us to deal with sin by admitting to God that we are sinners and throwing ourselves on his mercy, making use of the reconciliation that is now possible through Jesus. This act of confession is more than just telling God the facts of our situation, of course. The type of confession John is talking about flows from a penitent heart. There is no room here for the kind of "confession" that says "I can do whatever I want on Saturday night because Sunday morning I will confess and be forgiven." That is to use God's grace as a license for sin and is strongly condemned (see our discussion on Romans 6 above). The proper confessional attitude is exemplified by a tax collector in one of Jesus' parables:

> To some who were confident of their own righteousness and looked down on everybody else, Jesus told this parable: "Two men went up to the temple to pray, one a Pharisee and the other a tax collector. The Pharisee stood up and prayed about himself: 'God, I thank you that I am not like other men – robbers, evildoers, adulterers – or even like this tax collector. I fast twice a week and give a tenth of all I get.'
>
> "But the tax collector stood at a distance. He would not even look up to heaven, but beat his breast and said, 'God, have mercy on me, a sinner.'
>
> "I tell you that this man, rather than the other, went home justified before God. For everyone who exalts himself will be humbled, and he who humbles himself will be exalted." (Luke 18:9-14)

Everyone who confesses their sins in the manner of the tax collector will have those sins forgiven. John wants us to know that. However, as soon as he has made that point, he makes sure that we understand that this concession to the reality of sin is not a license to continue in sin. Right after explaining confession, John goes back to his main point: don't sin. Although we have an avenue for forgiveness in the event of sin, the bottom line is that a lifestyle of sin is a mark of an unbeliever and must not be tolerated by a follower of Christ. The very next passage in the epistle makes this clear:

> We know that we have come to know him if we obey his commands. The man who says, "I know him," but does not do what he commands is a liar, and the truth is not in him. But if anyone obeys his word, God's love is truly made complete in him. This is how we know we are in him: Whoever claims to live in him must walk as Jesus did. (1 John 2:3-6)

Nobody is perfect. However, we should all be striving for perfection. Becoming holy is a process, and the mark of a true believer is progressively greater righteousness. We may not be completely righteous, but we should be becoming more and more righteous. This is the point Peter makes in the passage with which we concluded the last chapter:

> Make every effort to add to your faith goodness; and to goodness, knowledge; and to knowledge, self-control; and to self-control, perseverance; and to perseverance, godliness; and to godliness, brotherly kindness; and to brotherly kindness, love. For if you possess these qualities in increasing measure, they will keep you from being ineffective and unproductive in your knowledge of our Lord Jesus Christ. (2 Peter 1:5-8)

We should have Paul's attitude:

But whatever was to my profit I now consider loss for the sake of Christ. What is more, I consider everything a loss compared to the surpassing greatness of knowing Christ Jesus my Lord, for whose sake I have lost all things. I consider them rubbish, that I may gain Christ and be found in him, not having a righteousness of my own that comes from the law, but that which is through faith in Christ – the righteousness that comes from God and is by faith. I want to know Christ and the power of his resurrection and the fellowship of sharing in his sufferings, becoming like him in his death, and so, somehow, to attain to the resurrection from the dead.

Not that I have already obtained all this, or have already been made perfect, but I press on to take hold of that for which Christ Jesus took hold of me. Brothers, I do not consider myself yet to have taken hold of it. But one thing I do: Forgetting what is behind and straining toward what is ahead, I press on toward the goal to win the prize for which God has called me heavenward in Christ Jesus. (Philippians 3:7-14)

Paul was striving to be perfect. He had not become perfect yet, but nothing less would satisfy. Paul wanted to be like Christ.

Sinful acts are symptomatic of an improper heart condition and constant exhibition of these acts without confession and repentance shows that a person is not being changed. On the other hand, a righteous person is continually growing in holiness and is truly repentant when sin occurs. In fact, a penitent heart shows that one is truly hungering and thirsting for righteousness.

Jesus came to free us not only from the penalty of sin, but from the power of sin as well. He wants to make you and me into a certain type of person. That is what the journey is all about.

Righteousness is not optional in the plan of redemption. Unfortunately, many people seem to think it is. A.W. Pink bemoaned the situation early in the twentieth century, and his critique is still valid.

> The nature of Christ's salvation is woefully misrepresented by the present-day evangelist. He announces a Savior from Hell rather than a Savior from sin. And that is why so many are fatally deceived, for there are multitudes who wish to escape the Lake of fire who have no desire to be delivered from their carnality and worldliness.[26]

We will close this chapter with a quotation from the great preacher, Charles Spurgeon, who also emphasized the necessity of righteousness:

> Christ will be master of the heart, and sin must be mortified. If your life is unholy, then your heart is unchanged, and you are an unsaved person. The Savior will sanctify His people, renew them, give them a hatred of sin, and a love of holiness. The grace that does not make a man better than others is a worthless counterfeit. Christ saves His people, not IN their sins, but FROM their sins. Without holiness, no man shall see the Lord.[27]

CHAPTER 10

The Necessity of Perseverance

We have come to share in Christ if we hold firmly till the end the confidence we had at first. As has just been said: "Today, if you hear his voice, do not harden our hearts as you did in the rebellion." Who were they who heard and rebelled? Were they not all those Moses led out of Egypt? And with whom was he angry for forty years? Was it not with those who sinned, whose bodies fell in the desert? And to whom did God swear that they would never enter his rest if not to those who disobeyed? So we see that they were not able to enter, because of their unbelief.

HEBREWS 3:14-19

You need to persevere so that when you have done the will of God, you will receive what he has promised.

HEBREWS 10:36

B ecause it is such an important episode in the Exodus story, I want to use this chapter to speak more about the Israelites' worship of the golden calf. Last chapter I described their problem as "falling into sin" and warned that sin must be avoided because it leads to death. I want to make essentially the same point in this chapter, but in two slightly different ways, corresponding to two slightly different ways of describing what happened at the base of Mount Sinai. Along with explaining the Israelites' rebellion as "falling into sin," we can also say that they "failed to make it to the end of the journey" and they "failed to be prepared for Moses' return from the top of the mountain." These distinctions are subtle, but I think this chapter will show you the value in making them. The biblical authors certainly saw it. They consistently referenced the story of the disobedient Israelites in warning us to persevere all the way to the end of our journey and to be prepared for the return of Christ. We will first look at biblical exhortations to persevere, followed by warnings to be ready.

Biblical Exhortations to Persevere

Sin separates from God. Whether we have never walked with God or have journeyed far toward the Promised Land, this law of the universe still applies. For this reason, we must constantly be on guard against sin, because the devil wants nothing more than to knock us off the narrow path. According to Peter, he "prowls around like a roaring lion looking for someone to devour" (1 Peter 5:8). As such, the Bible is filled with warnings to persevere in the battle and finish the race. We are to "resist him, standing firm in the faith" (1 Peter 5:9).

We have already seen the call to perseverance in 2 Peter 1:3-11 (at the end of Chapter 8), and 1 Corinthians 10:1-12 (at the beginning of Chapter 9); there are many more passages that make the same point. For example, the writer of Hebrews looks back at how the Israelites allowed sin to side-track them as part of his argument encouraging his readers to "hold on to the courage of which we boast" (Hebrews 3:6):

> So, as the Holy Spirit says: "Today, if you hear his voice, do not harden your hearts as you did in the rebellion, during the time of testing in the desert, where your fathers tested and tried me and for forty years saw what I did. That is why I was angry with that generation, and I said, 'Their hearts are always going astray, and they have not known my ways.' So I declared on oath in my anger, 'They shall never enter my rest.'"

> See to it, brothers, that none of you has a sinful, unbelieving heart that turns away from the living God. But encourage one another daily, as long as it is called Today, so that none of you may be hardened by sin's deceitfulness. We have come to share in Christ if we hold firmly till the end the confidence we had at first. As has just been said: "Today, if you hear his voice, do not harden your hearts as you did in the rebellion."

> Who were they who heard and rebelled? Were they not all those Moses led out of Egypt? And with whom was he angry for forty years? Was it not with those who sinned, whose bodies fell in the desert? And to whom did God swear that they would never enter his rest if not to those who disobeyed? So we see that they were not able to enter, because of their unbelief. (Hebrews 3:7-19)

The author then admonishes us to take heed and do better than the Israelites who did not enter the Promised Land. "Therefore, since the promise of entering his rest still stands, let us be careful that none of you be found to have fallen short of it" (Hebrews 4:1). He concludes by encouraging us to "hold firmly to the faith we profess" (Hebrews 4:14).

In the next chapter, the warnings about falling away from the faith become even more explicit:

> We have much to say about this, but it is hard to explain because you are slow to learn. In fact, though by this time you ought to be teachers, you need someone to teach you the elementary truths of God's word all over again. You need milk, not solid food! Anyone who lives on milk, being still an infant, is not acquainted with the teaching about righteousness. But solid food is for the mature, who by constant use have trained themselves to distinguish good from evil.

> Therefore let us leave the elementary teachings about Christ and go on to maturity, not laying again the foundation of repentance from acts that lead to death, and of faith in God, instruction about baptisms, the laying on of hands, the resurrection of the dead, and eternal judgment. And God permitting, we will do so.

> It is impossible for those who have once been enlightened, who have tasted the heavenly gift, who have shared in the Holy Spirit, who have tasted the goodness of the word of God and the powers of the coming age, if they fall away, to be brought back to repentance, because to their loss they are crucifying the Son of God all over again and subjecting him to public disgrace.

> Land that drinks in the rain often falling on it and that produces a crop useful to those for whom it is farmed receives the blessing of God. But land that produces thorns and thistles is worthless and is in danger of being cursed. In the end it will be burned.
>
> Even though we speak like this, dear friends, we are confident of better things in your case—things that accompany salvation. (Hebrews 5:11-6:9)

Although the writer is hopeful, the warnings are deadly serious. A life on the path of salvation always produces good fruits, which, as we have explained previously, are godly character qualities. A sojourner that fails to exhibit these qualities is in danger of being cursed. As is explained later in Hebrews, it will be dreadful for those God has to judge in this way:

> Let us draw near to God with a sincere heart in full assurance of faith, having our hearts sprinkled to cleanse us from a guilty conscience and having our bodies washed with pure water. Let us hold unswervingly to the hope we profess, for he who promised is faithful. And let us consider how we may spur one another on toward love and good deeds. Let us not give up meeting together, as some are in the habit of doing, but let us encourage one another—and all the more as you see the Day approaching.
>
> If we deliberately keep on sinning after we have received the knowledge of the truth, no sacrifice for sins is left, but only a fearful expectation of judgment and of raging fire that will consume the enemies of God. Anyone who rejected the law of Moses died without mercy on the testimony of two or three witnesses. How much more severely do you think a man deserves to

be punished who has trampled the Son of God under foot, who has treated as an unholy thing the blood of the covenant that sanctified him, and who has insulted the Spirit of grace? For we know him who said, "It is mine to avenge; I will repay," and again, "The Lord will judge his people." It is a dreadful thing to fall into the hands of the living God.

Remember those earlier days after you had received the light, when you stood your ground in a great contest in the face of suffering. Sometimes you were publicly exposed to insult and persecution; at other times you stood side by side with those who were so treated. You sympathized with those in prison and joyfully accepted the confiscation of your property, because you knew that you yourselves had better and lasting possessions.

So do not throw away your confidence; it will be richly rewarded. You need to persevere so that when you have done the will of God, you will receive what he has promised. For in just a very little while, "He who is coming will come and will not delay. But my righteous one will live by faith. And if he shrinks back, I will not be pleased with him." But we are not of those who shrink back and are destroyed, but of those who believe and are saved. (Hebrew 10:22-39)

Hopefully so. Races must be finished and battles must be won. There is no consolation prize for those who don't make it to the end of a journey and to finish second in war is to lose. There is no Promised Land for those who don't persevere in righteousness. After giving many examples of great heroes of faith who persevered even in the face of great persecution, the writer of Hebrews sums up the call: "Therefore, since we are surrounded by such a great cloud of witnesses, let us throw off everything that hinders and the sin that so easily entangles, and let us run with perseverance the race marked out for us" (Hebrews 12:1).

John exhorts,

> See that what you have heard from the beginning remains in you. If it does, you also will remain in the Son and in the Father. And this is what he promised us – even eternal life.
>
> I am writing these things to you about those who are trying to lead you astray. As for you, the anointing you received from him remains in you, and you do not need anyone to teach you. But as his anointing teaches you about all things and as that anointing is real, not counterfeit—just as it has taught you, remain in him. (1 John 2:24-29)

To remain in Jesus is to follow him and not turn back. As Jesus explained to a would-be disciple, Heaven is not for quitters. A man came to Jesus and said, "'I will follow you, Lord; but first let me go back and say good bye to my family.' Jesus replied, 'No one who puts his hand to the plow and looks back is fit for service in the kingdom of God'" (Luke 9:61-62).

Later in Luke we find Jesus warning his listeners that becoming a disciple is not a short-term commitment. Following Jesus requires following him to the end. Jesus told the people crowding around him to examine themselves and decide if they were willing to do that. Jesus asks, "If you start this, will you be able to finish it?"

> Large crowds were traveling with Jesus, and turning to them he said: "If anyone comes to me and does

not hate his father and mother, his wife and children, his brothers and sisters—yes, even his own life—he cannot be my disciple. And anyone who does not carry his cross and follow me cannot be my disciple.

"Suppose one of you wants to build a tower. Will he not first sit down and estimate the cost to see if he has enough money to complete it? For if he lays the foundation and is not able to finish it, everyone who sees it will ridicule him, saying, 'This fellow began to build and was not able to finish.'

"Or suppose a king is about to go to war against another king. Will he not first sit down and consider whether he is able with ten thousand men to oppose the one coming against him with twenty thousand? If he is not able, he will send a delegation while the other is still a long way off and will ask for terms of peace. In the same way, any of you who does not give up everything he has cannot be my disciple.

"Salt is good, but if it loses its saltiness, how can it be made salty again? It is fit neither for the soil nor for the manure pile; it is thrown out.

"He who has ears to hear, let him hear." (Luke 14:25-35)

Notice the salt reference at the end. Disciples of Jesus can start out salty but lose their flavor and become useless. No wonder Jesus said to "Listen up." This is very serious stuff.

Paul was so concerned about it that he openly worried that he might have wasted his efforts with the believers in Galatia.

Formerly, when you did not know God, you were slaves to those who by nature are not gods. But now that you know God – or rather are known by God – how is it that you are turning back to those weak and miserable principles? Do you wish to be enslaved by them all over again? You are observing special days and months and seasons and years! I fear for you, that somehow I have wasted my efforts on you. (Galatians 4:8-11)

Apparently the Galatians had been "running a good race," but now someone had "cut in on them" (Galatians 5:7) and "thrown them into confusion" (Galatians 5:10). After then describing the characteristics of a righteous person (the fruits of the Spirit, which we covered in Chapter 8), Paul emphasizes why they need to persevere in righteousness:

Do not be deceived: God cannot be mocked. A man reaps what he sows. The one who sows to please his sinful nature, from that nature will reap destruction; the one who sows to please the Spirit, from the Spirit will reap eternal life. Let us not become weary in doing good, for at the proper time we will reap a harvest if we do not give up. Therefore, as we have opportunity, let us do good to all people, especially to those who belong to the family of believers. (Galatians 6:7-10)

We must persevere in becoming righteous and not give up. As Paul told Titus, "The Lord delivered his people out of Egypt, but later destroyed those who did not believe" (Titus 6). We must not be like those Israelites. We are to "fight the good fight" and "hold on to faith and a good conscience" (1 Timothy 1:18-19), not "shipwreck our faith" as others have done (1 Timothy 1:20). "If we endure, we will also reign with him. If we disown him, he will also disown us; if we are faithless, he will remain faithful, for he cannot disown himself" (2 Timothy 2:12-13).

The Return of Moses and the Return of Christ

In our discussion of the Israelites' lapse into idolatry at the foot of Mount Sinai, we have looked at explicit biblical warnings against sin (Chapter 9) and admonitions to persevere in righteousness to the end of the journey (the first part of this chapter). The Hebrews failed on both counts when they worshipped the golden calf. They fell into sin and did not make it into the Promised Land. Now I want to talk about a third way to understand their failure: They were not ready for Moses' return.

As we already read, much of the impetus for building the calf came from impatience with Moses. The Israelites didn't have anybody watching over them, so they went their own way: "When the people saw that Moses was so long in coming down from the mountain, they gathered around Aaron and said, 'Come, make us gods who will go before us. As for this fellow Moses who brought us up out of Egypt, we don't know what has happened to him'" (Exodus 32:1). Aaron relented, and the Israelites were subsequently unprepared to meet Moses when he finally did come down the mountain.

This is another episode in which Moses is a type of Christ. Just as the Children of Israel should have remained faithful and been ready for Moses' return, we are to be ready for Jesus when he comes back. The Bible assures us that, just as Moses came down from the mountain and meted out justice, Jesus will return to earth and do the same. In the spirit of some of the great judgment days of the past, the return of Christ will be unexpected and severe:

Just as it was in the days of Noah, so also will it be in the days of the Son of Man. People were eating, drinking, marrying and being given in marriage up to the day Noah entered the ark. Then the flood came and destroyed them all.

It was the same in the days of Lot. People were eating and drinking, buying and selling, planting and building. But the day Lot left Sodom, fire and sulfur rained down from heaven and destroyed them all.

It will be just like this on the day the Son of Man is revealed. On that day no one who is on the roof of his house, with his goods inside, should go down to get them. Likewise, no one in the field should go back for anything. Remember Lot's wife! Whoever tries to keep his life will lose it, and whoever loses his life will preserve it. I tell you, on that night two people will be in one bed; one will be taken and the other left. Two women will be grinding grain together; one will be taken and the other left. (Luke 17:26-35)

The biblical authors use the fact of Christ's return as one more motivation for persevering in righteousness. For example, just after the passages we already read in 1 John that warn of the inherent dangers of sin and appeal to us to "remain in Jesus" (1 John 2:27), John makes the same plea with a slightly different impetus. This time he emphasizes that Jesus is coming back, and we don't want to be caught unprepared and ashamed on that day: "And now, dear children, continue in him, so that when he appears we may be confident and unashamed before him at his coming" (1 John 2:28).

Two Kinds of Readiness for Two Types of Events

Before we examine more biblical passages that warn us to be ready, I think it will be helpful to look briefly at the nature of readiness. Readiness is about being prepared for a future event. However, different categories of events require different types of readiness. We need to understand what type of event the coming of Jesus is so that we can prepare for it accordingly. I think there are many people who think they are ready to meet Jesus but simply are not because they have been preparing for the wrong kind of event.

There are at least two categories of future events. The first I will call the "Natural Disaster" category. This type of event would include earthquakes, hurricanes, and floods. To prepare for these events, people might do such tasks as secure bookshelves, reinforce walls and over-passes, board up windows, build up levees, purchase insurance, and perhaps evacuate if given enough warning.

There are two things to notice about the events in this category. The first is that preparing for them involves doing jobs that can be completed. The work required for preparation can be finished. You can reach a point where you just sit back and say, "I am prepared, at least as prepared as I want to be." For example, the hurricane is coming, but everyone in the city has evacuated and is sitting in hotel rooms 500 miles away, watching the coverage on TV, doing nothing but waiting.

The second thing to notice is that unless you go and undo what has already been done, you never become unready. People who are prepared for the storm remain ready while doing nothing more. Sitting in the hotel room just watching TV is not going to cause you to become less prepared. The windows stay boarded. After the checklist is completed, your readiness level remains the same. If the pantry has been filled with non-perishable food and medical supplies, it stays filled. It does not need to be continually re-stocked as you wait for an earthquake.

Of course, natural disasters are not the only type of events that fit into this category. Think about being ready for a vacation. The car is serviced and full of gas, the bags are packed, the travel insurance purchased, the route mapped out, the dog sitter scheduled, and the passport renewed. Every task on the pre-trip checklist is finished, and you are able to relax on the couch the night before the trip and say "I am prepared." The same principles apply. You were able to finish all the tasks, and are not going to become unready as you sit on the couch or sleep. Preparation is done. Now you just wait.

The second type of events fall into what I am going to call the "Unscheduled Return of the Boss to Work" category. A typical future event of this type would be the return of a supervisor from vacation or lunch at an undisclosed time. What does it take to be ready? Keeping busy. In order to be prepared for this event, you need to be sure to have enough work to do and then you need to keep doing it. The key to being ready when the boss pops in is to not be slacking off.

Here is what to notice about being ready for this category of events. First, it involves tasks that must be continually performed until the event occurs. You need to work at being ready right up until the time it happens. The job is never completed. You can never rest and must always be vigilant.

Although there are tasks involved that can be completed, such as upgrading the computer so it won't crash or making coffee to drink to keep energized, finishing those tasks only enables you to continue working. There's no saying to the boss "I *was* working but my printer ran out of ink, so I quit." Nor would it be wise to say, "I filled up the ink cartridges on the printer and figured that was good enough, so I called it a day." In both cases the manager will consider you unready for his or her return.

In this category of events there is no point where you can say, "I'm finished. I've done all I can. I am now completely ready for the person in charge to return." Instead, it is necessary to watch, to work, and to be prepared to watch and work for the long haul.

The second thing to notice about readiness for these types of events is that you can be ready at one point and then stop being ready. As long as you are performing the necessary tasks, you are ready, but as soon as you stop working, you become unready. Have you ever stayed busy right up until two minutes before your supervisor came back and then decided that one quick game of computer solitaire wouldn't hurt? You may have been ready up until two minutes before his or her return, but if the boss caught you playing cards, you weren't ready.

Another example of a future event that fits into this category is a terrorist attack. How do airports, for example, or buildings such as the White House prepare for a potential attack from terrorists? While they do some tasks that can be completed, such as installing concrete road blocks to keep cars at a distance, ultimately they would be less than secure if they did not also post guards to keep watch. These sentries are responsible to keep an around-the-clock lookout for suspicious activity. If the watchmen fall asleep on the job or don't show up for work, places like airports and the White House stop being ready. The same principle of readiness applies.

A final example of an "Unscheduled Return of the Boss" type of event is a bridal entrance. To be ready for a bride to make her appearance at a wedding, you have to be watching for her. You may have already accomplished many tasks to be ready for that moment (showering, traveling to the wedding site, purchasing a gift, etc.), but if you are not watching for the bride to enter, you are not ready.

This actually happened to me recently. My wife and I attended an outdoor wedding in a beautiful Southern

California location. We found our seats among a large group of old friends that we had not seen for a while, and everyone started visiting. Because of the acoustics of the setting, the music accompanying the ceremony was very hard to hear, and in the midst of our talking and laughing, we did not notice the wedding start. By the time we realized what was happening, most of the wedding party had already marched down the aisle and was waiting at the front for the bride. As everyone stood up to welcome her, we finally took notice. We were not ready, much to our embarrassment.

So again, readiness for this type of event involves tasks that must be continually performed until the event occurs. One must work at being prepared right up until the time the event happens. The work is never completed. There is no rest; one must always be vigilant.

That difference between the two categories of events is clearly seen in the answer to the question: "How do we know we are ready for a future event?" In the "Natural Disaster" category we would say, "We have accomplished certain tasks" or at least, "Certain tasks have already been accomplished." In the "Boss Returning to Work" category we would say, "We have performed certain tasks or certain tasks have been accomplished, *and* we are performing certain tasks and are prepared to perform them (or at least have them performed) indefinitely."

The Big Question

With this understanding of the nature of readiness as a background, we come to the big question: Which type of event is the return of Christ?

People often speak of Jesus' return as if it was a natural disaster. They talk of being ready using references to things accomplished in the past: "Jesus died for me. I asked him into my heart. Both of these events are done. My insurance is purchased, my windows are boarded up, and my book-shelves are securely fastened to the wall. I'm ready. I can rest. Hurricane Jesus is on the way, but all that can be done is done. I will be spared."

Jesus, however, never talked about being ready for his return in this sense. He never spoke of himself as anything like a hurricane or referred to being prepared for his return as if it was some kind of natural disaster. He did, however, in the context of teaching about his return, often refer to himself as a master, a thief and a bridegroom, metaphors that coincide precisely with being a boss, a terrorist and a bride. According to Jesus, his return fits perfectly into our second category of future events.

For example, in warning his disciples about the coming judgment at his return, Jesus compared himself to a master of household servants:

> No one knows about that day or hour, not even the angels in heaven, nor the Son, but only the Father. Be on guard! Be alert! You do not know when that time will come. It's like a man going away: He leaves his house and puts his servants in charge, each with his assigned task, and tells the one at the door to keep watch.
>
> Therefore keep watch because you do not know when the owner of the house will come back – whether in the evening, or at midnight, or when the rooster crows, or at dawn. If he comes suddenly, do not let him find you sleeping. What I say to you, I say to everyone: 'Watch!' (Mark 13:32-37)

It is clear which type of event this is. Jesus is the boss making an unscheduled return.

In a similar warning, Jesus compared himself to a thief in the night. The arrival of a burglar is to be treated exactly as we would treat a terrorist attack: with constant watchfulness:

> Therefore keep watch, because you do not know on what day your Lord will come. But understand this: If the owner of the house had known at what time of night the thief was coming, he would have kept watch and would not have let his house be broken into. So you also must be ready, because the Son of Man will come at an hour when you do not expect him. (Matthew 24:42-44)

Jesus then proceeded immediately to another story in which he is the master returning to his servants.

> Who then is the faithful and wise servant, whom the master has put in charge of the servants in his household to give them their food at the proper time? It will be good for that servant whose master finds him doing so when he returns. I tell you the truth, he will put him in charge of all his possessions. But suppose that servant is wicked and says to himself, "My master is staying away a long time," and he then begins to beat his fellow servants and to eat and drink with drunkards. The master of that servant will come on a day when he does not expect him and at an hour he is not aware of. He will cut him to pieces and assign him a place with the hypocrites, where there will be weeping and gnashing of teeth. (Matthew 24:45-51)

Then, just in case his listeners had not yet apprehended the point, Jesus compared himself to a bridegroom, another person whose coming must be prepared for with constant vigilance.

At that time the kingdom of heaven will be like ten virgins who took their lamps and went out to meet the bridegroom. Five of them were foolish and five were wise. The foolish ones took their lamps but did not take any oil with them. The wise, however, took oil in jars along with their lamps. The bridegroom was a long time in coming, and they all became drowsy and fell asleep.

At midnight the cry rang out: "Here's the bridegroom! Come out to meet him!"

Then all the virgins woke up and trimmed their lamps. The foolish ones said to the wise, "Give us some of your oil; our lamps are going out."

"No," they replied, "there may not be enough for both us and you. Instead, go to those who sell oil and buy some for yourselves."

But while they were on their way to buy the oil, the bridegroom arrived. The virgins who were ready went in with him to the wedding banquet. And the door was shut.

Later the others also came. "Sir! Sir!" they said. "Open the door for us!"

But he replied, "I tell you the truth, I don't know you."

Therefore keep watch, because you do not know the day or the hour. (Matthew 25:1-13)

In one teaching episode, Jesus used all the metaphors. He pulled together images of a boss and a thief and even threw in a reference to a wedding banquet, perhaps to remind his listeners of his other lessons on this subject.

"Be dressed ready for service and keep your lamps burning, like men waiting for their master to return from a wedding banquet, so that when he comes and knocks they can immediately open the door for him. It will be good for those servants whose master finds them watching when he comes. I tell you the truth, he will dress himself to serve, will have them recline at the table and will come and wait on them. It will be good for those servants whose master finds them ready, even if he comes in the second or third watch of the night. But understand this: If the owner of the house had known at what hour the thief was coming, he would not have let his house be broken into. You also must be ready, because the Son of Man will come at an hour when you do not expect him."

Peter asked, "Lord, are you telling this parable to us, or to everyone?"

The Lord answered, "Who then is the faithful and wise manager, whom the master puts in charge of his servants to give them their food allowance at the proper time? It will be good for that servant whom the master finds doing so when he returns. I tell you the truth, he will put him in charge of all his possessions. But suppose the servant says to himself, 'My master is taking a long time in coming,' and he then begins to beat the menservants and maidservants and to eat and drink and get drunk. The master of that servant will come on a day when he does not expect him and at an hour he is not aware of. He will cut him to pieces and assign him a place with the unbelievers." (Luke 12:35-46)

In all of his teachings, Jesus spoke of his return as an event that belongs in our second category. There is not a single example of Jesus telling us to prepare for his return as though it is natural disaster type of event. We are not to prepare as if the coming of Jesus is like a hurricane or earthquake, but rather as if the returning Jesus is like a thief or a boss coming back to the jobsite. Jesus tells his followers to be continually working, always watching, constantly on guard. Disciples are to never stop doing this; they are not to fall asleep. To be ready for Jesus means to keep busy until he returns, not rely on past actions. There is no point at which anyone can say, "I have done everything I need to do to be ready, and my preparation is complete." Rather, we must persevere in our work to the end.

The rest of the New Testament echoes the Gospels in teaching this principle. For example, Paul told the Thessalonians, "Now, brothers, about times and dates we do not need to write to you, for you know very well that the day of the Lord will come like a thief in the night. While people are saying, 'Peace and safety,' destruction will come on them suddenly, as labor pains on a pregnant woman, and they will not escape" (1 Thessalonians 5:1-3).

Being ready for Jesus is not a matter of having a nice list of past experiences to refer back to. It is a matter of working and watching for Him right now. It is a matter of growing in righteousness until the very moment we die or he returns. It means not falling asleep on the job. Living holy lives to the end is essential. Peter paints a very clear picture:

But the day of the Lord will come like a thief. The heavens will disappear with a roar; the elements will be destroyed by fire, and the earth and everything in it will be laid bare.

Since everything will be destroyed in this way, what kind of people ought you to be? You ought to live holy and godly lives as you look forward to the day of God and speed its coming. That day will bring about the destruction of the heavens by fire, and the elements will melt in the heat. But in keeping with his promise we are looking forward to a new heaven and a new earth, the home of righteousness.

So then, dear friends, since you are looking forward to this, make every effort to be found spotless, blameless and at peace with him. Bear in mind that our Lord's patience means salvation, just as our dear brother Paul also wrote you with the wisdom that God gave him. He writes the same way in all his letters, speaking in them of these matters. His letters contain some things that are hard to understand, which ignorant and unstable people distort, as they do the other Scriptures, to their own destruction.

Therefore, dear friends, since you already know this, be on your guard so that you may not be carried away by the error of lawless men and fall from your secure position. But grow in the grace and knowledge of our Lord and Savior Jesus Christ. To him be glory both now and forever! Amen. (2 Peter 3:10-18)

The potential for falling from a secure position is exactly what worried Jesus about the church in Sardis. He declared through John that they needed to wake up and follow the example of those who overcome and do not get their names blotted out of the Book of Life.

To the angel of the church in Sardis write: These are the words of him who holds the seven spirits of God and the seven stars. I know your deeds; you have a reputation of being alive, but you are dead. Wake up! Strengthen what remains and is about to die, for I have not found your deeds complete in the sight of my God. Remember, therefore, what you have received and heard; obey it, and repent. But if you do not wake up, I will come like a thief, and you will not know at what time I will come to you. Yet you have a few people in Sardis who have not soiled their clothes. They will walk with me, dressed in white, for they are worthy. He who overcomes will, like them, be dressed in white. I will never blot out his name from the book of life, but will acknowledge his name before my Father and his angels. He who has an ear, let him hear what the Spirit says to the churches. (Revelation 3:1-6)

Conclusion

The Israelites who worshipped the golden calf got their names blotted out of the book because they:

    a. Fell into sin
    b. Did not persevere to the end of the journey
    c. Were not prepared for Moses' return

These are, of course, just three ways of saying the same thing: sin is a very big deal at every stage in our journey and must be avoided at all costs. There will always be sin that needs to be confessed, as we discussed in Chapter 9, but we should constantly be growing in holiness. We should always be changing more and more into the type of person described in Chapter 8. We are not to let the length of the journey or its inherent hardships cause us to sin. As Jesus warned, don't let the things of this life keep you from being continually ready to meet him.

> Be careful, or your hearts will be weighed down with dissipation, drunkenness and the anxieties of life, and that day will close on you unexpectedly like a trap. For it will come upon all those who live on the face of the whole earth. Be always on the watch, and pray that you may be able to escape all that is about to happen, and that you may be able to stand before the Son of Man. (Luke 21:34-36)

Philosopher Dallas Willard rightly complains that today's church seems to spend a lot of time trying to get people's papers in order for heaven instead of fostering relationship with Jesus and true discipleship that results in holiness.[28] I hope that is not true of us. We don't want to be people (or be a church that produces people) who prepare for Jesus' return as if it was a hurricane. We don't want to be found on that great and mighty day of the Lord with a list of safety measures we completed years ago or an insurance contract in our hand saying, "Remember me? Remember when you signed this? I finished what you wanted me to do a long time ago. I'm sure glad I got that taken care of then and didn't have to do anything else because frankly, life got a little busy."

Instead, we want to be people who are able to greet Jesus as a benevolent master. When he appears, we should, setting aside what we have been doing for the kingdom, be able to run up to Jesus with a big hug and say, "I've been expecting you." We should be people who can rightly expect to hear him say, "I know my child. Well done, good and faithful servant."

CHAPTER 11

God with Us

The LORD replied, "My Presence will go with you, and I will give you rest."

EXODUS 33:14

The virgin will be with child and will give birth to a son, and they will call him Immanuel – which means, "God with us."

MATTHEW 1:23

The journey across the wilderness wasn't going very well for the Children of Israel. They failed badly when they didn't have food or water and then failed badly again in building a golden calf while Moses was on the mountain. By this point, God seemed to have had enough. He told Moses to continue leading the people to the Promised Land, but God was not going to go with them. He would send an angel instead.

> Then the LORD said to Moses, "Leave this place, you and the people you brought up out of Egypt, and

go up to the land I promised on oath to Abraham, Isaac and Jacob, saying, 'I will give it to your descendants.' I will send an angel before you and drive out the Canaanites, Amorites, Hittites, Perizzites, Hivites and Jebusites. Go up to the land flowing with milk and honey. But I will not go with you, because you are a stiff-necked people and I might destroy you on the way." (Exodus 33:1-3)

Moses doubted that he would be able to succeed on this mission and cried out to God in discouragement.

Moses said to the LORD, "You have been telling me, 'Lead these people,' but you have not let me know whom you will send with me. You have said, 'I know you by name and you have found favor with me.' If you are pleased with me, teach me your ways so I may know you and continue to find favor with you. Remember that this nation is your people." (Exodus 33:12-13)

I am sure we can understand Moses' frustration. The journey is long and hard, and humans seem ill-equipped to carry it out. The call to persevere in holiness that we discussed in the previous two chapters may have left you unsure about your prospects. "I don't think I can do it" seems to me a perfectly normal response. God understands this, just like he understood Moses' concern. In his grace, he gave Moses a helper: God himself.

The LORD replied, "My Presence will go with you, and I will give you rest."

Then Moses said to him, "If your Presence does not go with us, do not send us up from here. How will anyone know that you are pleased with me and with your people unless you go with us? What else will distinguish me and your people from all the other people on the face of the earth?"

And the LORD said to Moses, "I will do the very thing you have asked, because I am pleased with you and I know you by name." (Exodus 33:14-17)

God made success on the journey possible by actually coming down and traveling with the Israelites. In this chapter we will examine what that looked like and then see how God does the same thing for us.

God's Tabernacle

As sojourners in the wilderness, the Israelites obviously did not have any permanent dwellings in which to live. However, they did not leave themselves completely open to the elements. They carried along portable tent-like structures. These booths, or tabernacles, were basically poles covered by flexible material like cloth or animal hides. These shelters provided protection and easy portability.

When God decided to come and travel with the Israelites across the wilderness, he ordered them to build for him a portable structure to inhabit: his tabernacle (Exodus 25:8). You can find the explicit architectural instructions for this building in Exodus Chapters 25 through 30 and the account of the building process in Exodus Chapters 35 through 40. When they were finished, a cloud covered the tent "and the glory of the Lord filled the tabernacle" (Exodus 40:34).

The book of Exodus then concludes,

In all the travels of the Israelites, whenever the cloud lifted from above the tabernacle, they would set out;

but if the cloud did not lift, they did not set out – until the day it lifted. So the cloud of the LORD was over the tabernacle by day, and fire was in the cloud by night, in the sight of all the house of Israel during all their travels. (Exodus 40:36-38)

Although there is much we could say about the tabernacle, for our purposes I will focus on the fact that in order to get the people across the wilderness, God came down and dwelt in the same type of portable home as they were living in. He condescended to help the Israelites by leaving his heavenly home to reside with them in their temporary shelters.

God's presence provided the people with guidance and protection. With the cloud and the fire always in view over the tabernacle, they could be assured that they were safe and on the right track. If ever doubts arose about the chances of making it across the wilderness successfully, the people could gain assurance from the knowledge that God was with them.

The Feast of Tabernacles

In later years, after the Israelites were settled in the Promised Land, they were commanded to commemorate this aspect of the journey by holding the Festival of Tabernacles, also known as the Feast of Booths or *Sukkot* in Hebrew. (Deuteronomy 16:13-15). Here are God's directions for the festival as recorded in Leviticus.

So beginning with the fifteenth day of the seventh month, after you have gathered the crops of the land, celebrate the festival to the LORD for seven days; the first day is a day of rest, and the eighth day also is a day of rest. On the first day you are to take choice fruit from the trees, and palm fronds, leafy branches and poplars, and rejoice before the LORD your God for seven days. Celebrate this as a festival to the LORD for seven days each year. This is to be a lasting ordinance for the generations to come; celebrate it in the seventh month. Live in booths for seven days: All native-born Israelites are to live in booths so your descendants will know that I had the Israelites live in booths when I brought them out of Egypt. I am the LORD your God. (Leviticus 23:39-43)

To this day certain Jews celebrate the Festival of Tabernacles by building portable huts outside their permanent homes and living in them for a full week. As they celebrate the harvest and God's continued provision and protection, they remember a time when God provided for them in temporary shelters and protected them when they were sojourners in the wilderness. They recall how God provided manna for them from Heaven and water from the rock, and they especially remember how God journeyed with them across the wilderness by inhabiting his own temporary shelter, his own tabernacle.

Jesus' Birthday

To begin my explanation of what all this information means to us, I am going to argue that Jesus was born on the first day of the Feast of Tabernacles. While I am not interested in canceling Christmas or giving up celebrating Jesus' birth in December each year, I think there are many good reasons to think it actually occurred on *Sukkot,* and that this date provides a depth of meaning to the event that December 25th simply does not.

Let's start by establishing the date of John the Baptist's birth with some simple number crunching. John's father Zechariah was a priest serving on duty in the temple when the angel Gabriel appeared to him to tell him that he would have a son (Luke 1:8). We know from Luke 1:5 that Zechariah belonged to the priestly division of Abijah. From this bit of information we can nail down almost exactly what time of year the angel appeared him and then deduce from that when Jesus was born. To do so, however, we will need some background in the Jewish priestly system.

Priests served in the temple in teams, with each team serving for one week at a time (1 Chronicles 9), two times a year. The teams were scheduled to serve in a certain order each year, and 1 Chronicles 24:7-18 explains that the division of Abijah was the 8th team of the year. This was called the eighth course.

Along with their two weeks of individual priestly service, all the priests would report to the temple and serve together three times a year during the Feast of Weeks, the Feast of Unleavened Bread and the Feast of Booths (Deuteronomy 16:16). The total number of weeks served in the temple by each priest, then, was five.

Because the Feast of Unleavened Bread and the Feast of Weeks both occur within the first eight weeks of the Jewish year, the eighth course would have served during the tenth week of the year (approximately Sivan 12-18). As such, the priestly division of Abijah would have started serving on the second Sabbath of Sivan and worked the following six days. We can surmise that this was the week of Gabriel's visit to Zechariah.

Assuming Zechariah's wife, Elizabeth, conceived John the Baptist soon after Zechariah had finished his Temple service, she would have become pregnant after the third Sabbath of Sivan (approximately Sivan 19-25).

Having a conception date for John allows us to figure out the birthday of Jesus because we know that the angel appeared to Mary to announce that she would bear Jesus when Elizabeth was six months pregnant (Luke 1:23-33).

This would have been Hanukkah, the Jewish Festival of Lights. If we assume that Jesus was conceived about the time of the angel's appearance, that would mean the "Light of the World" (John 1:9, 9:5, 11:9) was conceived during the Festival of Lights. This is just one "coincidental" image in what will become a long list before this chapter is over.

Three months after that, John the Baptist was born, about the time of Passover. This also may be more than coincidence because of the imagery found in the Seder meal. As part of this dinner, Jews place an empty chair at the table for Elijah, hoping that he will soon arrive and fulfill the prophecy of Malachi 4:5 that says that Elijah must return before the Messiah and prepare the way for him. So if our dates are correct, at just the time the Jews were praying for Elijah to return, John the Baptist was born, a man who Jesus said was in fact (at least symbolically) Elijah. Speaking of John, Jesus said, "And if you are willing to accept it, he is the Elijah who was to come" (Matthew 11:14).

Jesus was born six months after Passover, then, in autumn, right around the time of the Festival of Tabernacles.

What Jesus' Birth Date Means to Us

To begin to understand why the actual date of Jesus' birth is important, we need to realize that God often corresponds major historical events to other events in order to help us understand their significance. For instance, we already talked about how Jesus was killed on Passover so that we would better understand that he is the lamb that takes the punishment for sin. We won't go into detail here, but other events that similarly correspond to Jewish holidays would be Jesus' resurrection on the Feast of Firstfruits (Leviticus 23-14, 1 Corinthians 15:20-23), and the outpouring of the Holy Spirit at the Feast of Weeks (Leviticus 23:15-22, Acts 2), to name but two.

The significance of Jesus being born on the Feast of Tabernacles can be clearly seen when we realize that by descending to earth to take up residence in a human body, Jesus reenacted and fulfilled the act of God descending to earth in the wilderness to take up residence in a tent.

Just as the tabernacles were the temporary dwellings of the sojourning Israelites as they traveled to their permanent home, Canaan, our bodies are our temporary dwellings as we travel across the wilderness of life to our permanent home, Heaven. And just as God came down to help the Israelites along in their quest by living with them in the same type of tent as they were using, Jesus came down to help us along by living with us in the same type of tent that we use: a human body.

That is why John can say, "The Word became flesh and made his dwelling among us. We have seen his glory, the glory of the One and Only, who came from the Father, full of grace and truth" (John 1:14). The term "made his dwelling" in this verse is literally "tabernacled." It comes from the Greek word *skenos*, which means tent or tabernacle and refers to the Hebrew *sukkah*, the singular form of *Sukkot*. John is saying that in Jesus, God took up residence on earth in the same way he did in the desert. By becoming flesh, he set up his tabernacle in the midst of all the rest of the tabernacles so that he might get us through the wilderness. As Matthew explained, this was a fulfillment of a prophecy in Isaiah: "All this took place to fulfill what the Lord had said through the prophet: 'The virgin will be with child and will give birth to a son, and they will call him Immanuel – which means, "God with us"'" (Matthew 1:22-23).

The Holy Spirit

By now you might be thinking, "I see how Jesus could play the same role that God played in the desert, but Jesus is no longer with us. He no longer inhabits an earthly body, so what good will that do us today?" That is a fair question, and it leads us to a discussion of the Holy Spirit.

When Jesus was preparing to leave this world, he comforted his disciples by assuring them that they would not be left alone.

> And I will ask the Father, and he will give you another Counselor to be with you forever – the Spirit of truth. The world cannot accept him, because it neither sees him nor knows him. But you know him, for he lives with you and will be in you. I will not leave you as orphans; I will come to you. Before long, the world will not see me anymore, but you will see me. Because I live, you also will live. On that day you will realize that I am in my Father, and you are in me, and I am in you. (John 14:16-20)

After a brief discussion with Judas, he gave this counselor a name: The Holy Spirit. "All this I have spoken while still with you. But the Counselor, the Holy Spirit, whom the Father will send in my name, will teach you all things and will remind you of everything I have said to you" (John 14:25-26).

Jesus was telling the disciples that they need not worry because when the Holy Spirit comes, God will not just be dwelling in *a* human body, but he will be dwelling in *their* human body. God will actually take up residence inside of them. They will be the tabernacle, or as Paul describes it, God's temple: "Don't you know that you yourselves are God's temple and that God's Spirit lives in you?" (1 Corinthians 3:16).

Jesus described the duties of the Holy Spirit more fully later in the same discourse.

But I tell you the truth: It is for your good that I am going away. Unless I go away, the Counselor will not come to you; but if I go, I will send him to you. When he comes, he will convict the world of guilt in regard to sin and righteousness and judgment: in regard to sin, because men do not believe in me; in regard to righteousness, because I am going to the Father, where you can see me no longer; and in regard to judgment, because the prince of this world now stands condemned.

I have much more to say to you, more than you can now bear. But when he, the Spirit of truth, comes, he will guide you into all truth. He will not speak on his own; he will speak only what he hears, and he will tell you what is yet to come. He will bring glory to me by taking from what is mine and making it known to you. All that belongs to the Father is mine. That is why I said the Spirit will take from what is mine and make it known to you. (John 16:7-15)

Jesus was saying that just as God guided the Israelites during the Exodus and Jesus guided his disciples while on Earth, the Holy Spirit will guide believers after Jesus leaves. Because of this, followers of Jesus today can have hope. Although we have to live in temporary dwellings now, the fact that we have the Holy Spirit living in them with us should be an encouragement. The Holy Spirit provides us with the strength and wisdom to face whatever trials and troubles come our way. This was certainly Paul's argument to the struggling Corinthians. In the midst of a long admonition explaining why they are not to "lose heart" (2 Corinthians 4:1), he said,

Now we know that if the earthly tent [*skenos*] we live in is destroyed, we have a building from God, an eternal house in heaven, not built by human hands. Meanwhile we groan, longing to be clothed with our heavenly dwelling, because when we are clothed, we will not be found naked. For while we are in this tent, we groan and are burdened, because we do not wish to be unclothed but to be clothed with our heavenly dwelling, so that what is mortal may be swallowed up by life.

Now it is God who has made us for this very purpose and has given us the Spirit as a deposit, guaranteeing what is to come. (2 Corinthians 5:1-5)

The Water Libation Ceremony

Another ceremony that was performed during the Feast of Tabernacles (at least during the years that the Temple was in Jerusalem, which would have included Jesus' time) illuminates this truth. It was called the *Nisuch HaMayim*, or "Pouring of the Water." Every morning a priest carrying a golden pitcher led a procession to the pool of Siloam. The priest would fill the pitcher and bring it back through the water gate into Jerusalem and pour it into a receptacle on the altar. After they poured the water, the priests would march around the altar as the people sang the Hallel Psalms (Psalm 113-118) with special emphasis on Psalm 118:25: "O Lord, save us; O Lord, grant us success."

This ceremony was about asking God to bless the upcoming rainy season. It was very joyful, anticipatory and indeed, Messianic. They were thinking of God's miraculous provision of salvific water in the desert as they looked ahead to what God would do to save them in the future, not just from physical drought, but from all oppression. In this spirit, they would refer to Isaiah 12, particularly verse 3 (in italics).

> In that day you will say: "I will praise you, O LORD. Although you were angry with me, your anger has turned away and you have comforted me. Surely God is my salvation; I will trust and not be afraid. The LORD, the LORD, is my strength and my song; he has become my salvation."

> *With joy you will draw water from the wells of salvation.*

> In that day you will say: "Give thanks to the LORD, call on his name; make known among the nations what he has done, and proclaim that his name is exalted. Sing to the LORD, for he has done glorious things; let this be known to all the world. Shout aloud and sing for joy, people of Zion, for great is the Holy One of Israel among you." (Isaiah 12:1-6, emphasis mine)

The Messianic theme was especially strong on the last day of the feast, called *Hashanna Rabba* or the "Great Hosanna." The processional on this morning did not end with just one trip around the altar, but seven. As the priests encircled the sacred place and read Psalm 118, the people waved branches and echoed each line with a loud "Hallelujah." Then, starting in verse 25, they would join in with the phrase, "Hosanna, make your salvation now manifest, Oh Lord." It was a day of extremely joyful Messianic expectation. With this event as a backdrop, Jesus made a very special announcement, which the Apostle John interprets for us:

> On the last and greatest day of the Feast, Jesus stood
> and said in a loud voice, "If anyone is thirsty, let him
> come to me and drink. Whoever believes in me, as the
> Scripture has said, streams of living water will flow
> from within him." By this he meant the Spirit, whom
> those who believed in him were later to receive. Up
> to that time the Spirit had not been given, since Jesus
> had not yet been glorified. (John 7:37-39)

Just as the people are asking for the Messiah during the
biggest day of the Festival of Tabernacles, Jesus stood up
and said "Here I am! Are you thirsty for the water that will
provide eternal life? I am the source. I will send the Holy
Spirit to inhabit you." It is a wonderful image.

In explicitly comparing himself (and the Holy Spirit to
follow) to the water provided to the Israelites in the desert,
Jesus establishes imagery that was later expounded on by
Paul. In talking about the desert wanderers, he explains,
"They all ate the same spiritual food and drank the same
spiritual drink; for they drank from the spiritual rock that
accompanied them, and that rock was Christ" (1 Corinthians
10:3-4).

God will get us across the wilderness by dwelling with
us. He comes down and takes up residence in our temporary dwellings in order to guide, protect, and strengthen us
as we travel. He enables us to live righteously. Our hope for
getting safely home rests in the indwelling (tabernacling) of
the Holy Spirit in our bodies.

The Transfiguration

Another event in Jesus' life that may be connected to the
Festival of Tabernacles is the transfiguration.

After six days Jesus took Peter, James and John with him and led them up a high mountain, where they were all alone. There he was transfigured before them. His clothes became dazzling white, whiter than anyone in the world could bleach them. And there appeared before them Elijah and Moses, who were talking with Jesus.

Peter said to Jesus, "Rabbi, it is good for us to be here. Let us put up three shelters – one for you, one for Moses and one for Elijah." (He did not know what to say, they were so frightened.)

Then a cloud appeared and enveloped them, and a voice came from the cloud: "This is my Son, whom I love. Listen to him!"

Suddenly, when they looked around, they no longer saw anyone with them except Jesus.

As they were coming down the mountain, Jesus gave them orders not to tell anyone what they had seen until the Son of Man had risen from the dead. They kept the matter to themselves, discussing what "rising from the dead" meant. (Mark 9:2-10)

Jesus had been talking to his disciples about the resurrection and had been trying to convince them that this world is not the end and this body is not their permanent home. At the transfiguration he gave them some evidence for his claims. Not only did he appear to them in a glorified state, but he talked with Moses and Elijah, two dead guys! If life after this body is not possible, what were Moses and Elijah doing there? If their earthly bodies were their permanent home, they would not have been appearing with Jesus.

Peter offers to make some booths for them, which is the reason some scholars think this event took place during the Festival of Tabernacles. Whether it did or not, one of the points being made here is that Moses and Elijah no longer need booths. They no longer live in the temporary home that was their earthly body; they now live in their permanent home. I think they typify two types of people: those who die naturally (Moses, Deuteronomy 34:5) and those who are taken up by God without natural death (Elijah, 2 Kings 2:11). Whether we die naturally or Jesus comes and gets us, we will look back on this body as a temporary shelter for the journey, not our permanent home, and the transfiguration is a good evidence of that.

Peter certainly took this meaning from the event. In trying to encourage his readers to persevere, and fight the good fight, and make it through the wilderness, he said we can take hope in the assurance of our future glorification from the transfiguration. The transfiguration proved that this body is not all there is. Our permanent home awaits.

So I will always remind you of these things, even though you know them and are firmly established in the truth you now have. I think it is right to refresh your memory as long as I live in the tent [*skenos*] of this body, because I know that I will soon put it aside, as our Lord Jesus Christ has made clear to me. And I will make every effort to see that after my departure you will always be able to remember these things.

We did not follow cleverly invented stories when we told you about the power and coming of our Lord Jesus Christ, but we were eyewitnesses of his majesty. For he received honor and glory from God the Father when the voice came to him from the Majestic Glory, saying, "This is my Son, whom I love; with him I am well pleased." We ourselves heard this voice that came from heaven when we were with him on the sacred mountain. (2 Peter 1:12-18)

Water of Life for Everyone

Another aspect of the festival that is worth noting is the fact that it is the one festival that is open to everyone. One didn't have to be a Jew to take part. During the "waving of the four species" ceremony, for instance, four types of branches are bound together and waved in all directions (east, west, north, south, up, and down). While there are many levels of meaning to this ceremony, one reason for it is to represent God's mastery of all of creation and his care for all peoples of the world. God is everywhere and for everyone. He invites all to come and partake of the living water. He wants to tabernacle not only with the Jews, but with all people. God wants to send the Holy Spirit to indwell everyone and guide them home.

Zechariah adds some impetus to this invitation by explaining that all nations *must* come to the festival or they will be punished. But notice what the punishment is: they will not receive rain. Understanding that "rain" is symbolic of the Holy Spirit, God is saying that anyone who wants to make it across the wilderness needs the Holy Spirit and therefore must come, metaphorically, to the Festival of Booths.

> Then the survivors from all the nations that have attacked Jerusalem will go up year after year to worship the King, the LORD Almighty, and to celebrate the Feast of Tabernacles. If any of the peoples of the earth do not go up to Jerusalem to worship the King, the LORD Almighty, they will have no rain. If the Egyptian people do not go up and take part, they will have no rain. The LORD will bring on them the plague he inflicts on the nations that do not go up to

celebrate the Feast of Tabernacles. This will be the punishment of Egypt and the punishment of all the nations that do not go up to celebrate the Feast of Tabernacles. (Zechariah 14:16-19)

Those that do not go celebrate God's dwelling with us, who do not appropriate his gracious act, will not be blessed.

Joy to the World

The Festival of Tabernacles was the only festival with the explicit command to be joyful. In Bethlehem, to the singing of angels, God indwelt our tabernacle, our body. He dwelt with us and continues to do so today through the Holy Spirit, so that we might make it to the Promised Land. That makes it a merry Christmas, indeed.

PART III

Into the Promised Land

Practical Tips for a Successful Trip

CHAPTER 12

The Comfort Trap

Now the people complained about their hardships in the hearing of the LORD, and when he heard them his anger was aroused.

NUMBERS 11:1

Let us fix our eyes on Jesus, the author and perfecter of our faith, who for the joy set before him endured the cross, scorning its shame, and sat down at the right hand of the throne of God. Consider him who endured such opposition from sinful men, so that you will not grow weary and lose heart.

HEBREWS 12:1-3

Our biblical guidebook, Exodus, ends with the account of God indwelling the tabernacle. The story of the Israelites' journey to the Promised Land is completed in the final three books of Moses (Leviticus, Numbers and Deuteronomy). I want to highlight just two episodes from that part of the story as we conclude this book with two lessons about how to persevere to the end and arrive safely at home.

"Manna for Dinner Again?"

As we pick up the story in Numbers, we find that not even having God dwelling with them in the tabernacle kept the Israelites from grumbling against him.

> Now the people complained about their hardships in the hearing of the LORD, and when he heard them his anger was aroused. Then fire from the LORD burned among them and consumed some of the outskirts of the camp. When the people cried out to Moses, he prayed to the LORD and the fire died down. So that place was called Taberah, because fire from the LORD had burned among them. (Numbers 11:1-3)

Traveling across the wilderness was difficult. Living as nomads in the scorching desert with enemies all around isn't anybody's idea of a comfortable or pleasant existence. The Israelites didn't like it and they let God know. Unfortunately for them, God didn't see the value in their complaining and judgment fell. However, even that didn't stop the grumbling. "The rabble with them began to crave other food, and again the Israelites started wailing and said, 'If only we had meat to eat! We remember the fish we ate in Egypt at no cost – also the cucumbers, melons, leeks, onions and garlic. But now we have lost our appetite; we never see anything but this manna!'" (Numbers 11:4-6).

This didn't sit well with God, either. He gave Moses these instructions:

> "Tell the people: 'Consecrate yourselves in prepara-
> tion for tomorrow, when you will eat meat. The Lord

heard you when you wailed, "If only we had meat to eat! We were better off in Egypt!" Now the LORD will give you meat, and you will eat it. You will not eat it for just one day, or two days, or five, ten or twenty days, but for a whole month – until it comes out of your nostrils and you loathe it – because you have rejected the LORD, who is among you, and have wailed before him, saying, "Why did we ever leave Egypt?"" (Numbers 11:18-20)

Be careful what you wish for, the old saying goes, you just might get it.

Now a wind went out from the LORD and drove quail in from the sea. It brought them down all around the camp to about three feet above the ground, as far as a day's walk in any direction. All that day and night and all the next day the people went out and gathered quail. No one gathered less than ten homers. Then they spread them out all around the camp. But while the meat was still between their teeth and before it could be consumed, the anger of the Lord burned against the people, and he struck them with a severe plague. Therefore the place was named Kibroth Hattaavah, because there they buried the people who had craved other food. (Numbers 11:31-34)

So we have two more incidents in which God became angry and judged the people because of their grumbling. The Israelites complained first about general hardships and then about not having enough variety in their menu. They had griped about food before, of course, but notice the difference this time. When the Israelites complained previously about not having water to drink or bread to eat, they were concerned for their very survival – they were worried about dying in the desert. That was not a factor in this case, as there was plenty of food and water to keep the people nourished. This time they were after variety. The Israelites were tired of manna and wanted some meat. They were past looking for simply survival. They no longer wanted to just get by; they wanted prosperity.

Evaluating these two events together, we can summarize by saying that the Israelites were complaining because they wanted a higher degree of comfort than they were experiencing. They wanted a life with more ease and fancier food. They wanted more, to borrow a term from Francis Schaeffer, "personal peace and affluence."

> Personal peace means just to be let alone, not to be troubled by the troubles of other people, whether across the world or across the city – to live one's life with minimal possibilities of being personally disturbed. Personal peace means wanting to have my personal life pattern undisturbed in my lifetime, regardless of what the result will be in the lifetimes of my children and grandchildren. Affluence means an overwhelming and ever-increasing prosperity – a life made up of things, things, and more things – a success judged by an ever-higher level of material advance.[29]

Schaeffer aptly describes the longings of the Israelites. We see their desire for personal peace in their grumbling about "hardships." They no longer wanted to be disturbed by enemies, heat, sandstorms and all the other things that made the journey difficult. We see their desire for affluence in the request for meat. They were not content with the necessities of life; they wanted some luxuries.

The Problem with Choosing Personal Peace and Prosperity

So what is the problem? What is so wrong with a little peace and prosperity? Why did God get so angry with the Israelites?

The key to the answer is found in remembering their situation. The Israelites were in the midst of a journey and a battle. They were on a trip to the Promised Land that involved fighting against harsh conditions and human enemies. Like Sam and Frodo in *The Lord of the Rings*, the Israelites were traversing a tough land in order to reach a specific destination, all the while having to fend off attacks from a variety of adversaries. They were sojourners, and they were soldiers. Put another way, I think we could accurately label them athletes and warriors. They were striving to complete a race and win a fight. As such, the last thing the people should have been expecting is comfort. The reason for this, of course, is that to be a successful athlete or soldier, one has to sacrifice personal peace and prosperity. Athletes and soldiers have to give up comfort in order to gain victory.

For instance, think of what it takes to win the Tour de France. Riding a bicycle for hundreds of miles over multiple mountain passes is anything but comfortable. Muscles ache, lungs burn, and I am quite sure every part of the cyclist's body longs for it to be over. However, a champion must keep going through the pain. The only alternative is to lose. If, in the middle of the race, the rider chooses peace for his sore muscles by stopping, he doesn't win. It's as simple as that. If Sam and Frodo had decided to choose resting in The Shire rather than struggling through to Mordor and Mount Doom, all would have been lost.

Or think of what it takes to win a war. What could be less comfortable and peaceful for a soldier than a firefight? Yet victory requires that these battles be fought. To choose comfort in a war is to lose the war. Refusing to fight because the pain of battle is too great is simply to surrender. Personal peace must be sacrificed to win races and fights. Embracing hardship is essential to victory. The Israelites made the mistake of not doing that.

In regard to prosperity, the same principle holds true. Consider again what athletes and soldiers go through to gain success. While others are sleeping in, they are at the gym shooting baskets, in the pool swimming laps, or at the rifle range taking shots. While others are lounging in front of the television with a bowl of popcorn, they are in the weight room working out. While others are lazing at the beach, they are at summer training camp. Soldiers and athletes give up certain levels of prosperity in order to achieve a level of excellence that will lead them to victory. They deny themselves some extravagances and accept a more modest lifestyle because this type of discipline is necessary to win. Prosperity must be sacrificed for victory. The Israelites failed to do this as well. They fell into what I refer to as the comfort trap.

The Four Soils

The desire for personal peace and prosperity is one of the great obstacles to victory in the Christian life. The comfort trap keeps many people out of the Promised Land, as Jesus made plain in the parable of the soils:

> That same day Jesus went out of the house and sat by the lake. Such large crowds gathered around him that he got into a boat and sat in it, while all the people stood on the shore. Then he told them many things in parables, saying: "A farmer went out to sow his seed. As he was scattering the seed, some fell along the path, and the birds came and ate it up. Some fell on rocky places, where it did not have much soil. It sprang up quickly, because the soil was shallow. But

when the sun came up, the plants were scorched, and they withered because they had no root. Other seed fell among thorns, which grew up and choked the plants. Still other seed fell on good soil, where it produced a crop—a hundred, sixty or thirty times what was sown. He who has ears, let him hear." (Matthew 13:1-9)

Jesus went on to explain the parable.

> Listen then to what the parable of the sower means: When anyone hears the message about the kingdom and does not understand it, the evil one comes and snatches away what was sown in his heart. This is the seed sown along the path. The one who received the seed that fell on rocky places is the man who hears the word and at once receives it with joy. But since he has no root, he lasts only a short time. When trouble or persecution comes because of the word, he quickly falls away. The one who received the seed that fell among the thorns is the man who hears the word, but the worries of this life and the deceitfulness of wealth choke it, making it unfruitful. But the one who received the seed that fell on good soil is the man who hears the word and understands it. He produces a crop, yielding a hundred, sixty or thirty times what was sown. (Matthew 13:18-23)

The four types of soil are four types of people. All four hear the message of the Kingdom, and three start producing a crop. In other words, three start traveling across the wilderness, walking the narrow road. However, two of those three fail to finish the journey. Two of the three ultimately fail to produce fruit. What causes them to fail? According to Jesus, it is persecution (verse 21), the worries of this life, and the deceitfulness of wealth (verse 22). These people are brought down because they run into hardships in the form of persecution and day-to-day worries and they chase after material wealth, which can never satisfy. Notice what kept these people from the Kingdom. The soils that didn't produce fruit are those that chose *personal peace and prosperity* over Jesus. They chose comfort over truth, ease of life over victory. They were not good athletes or soldiers.

Peter exhibited these characteristics when Jesus was on trial. Even after vowing to stay with Jesus through thick and thin (Mark 14:29), Peter denied he even knew Jesus when the going got too tough (Mark 14:66-72). Peter was brought down by a desire for comfort in the midst of persecution. Of course, Peter later became one of the most courageous evangelists in the world and was ultimately martyred for his savior, but in the episode at Jesus' trial, he failed.

It is not easy to live as an athlete or soldier. It is not easy to live in discomfort. However, it can be done. Indeed, it must be done, but how?

Two Measures

There are two important measures we can take that are indispensable for persevering through discomfort and defeating the desire for personal peace and prosperity. First we need to remember that this world is not our home. Second, we need to keep focused on the goal: our true home, Heaven. Although these actions are basically two sides of the same coin, I think it is helpful to speak of them separately.

This World Is Not Our Home

First, remember that this world is not our home. Don't expect it to feel like home.

I have had the pleasure of speaking at a Bible Camp in northern Canada a couple of times. The camp is located in a beautiful spot, but frankly it is not a very comfortable place to stay. The cabins are old, the mosquitoes are massive, and the ground is covered in fine sand that gets everywhere. Everyone walks around in varying states of grubbiness all week. However, I had a wonderful time there; it never crossed my mind to complain about the conditions. In fact, I hardly ever heard a camper complain about them either.

The reason for this lack of concern about the conditions is, of course, that we were *camping*! Camping is not supposed to be comfortable. It is not supposed to have all the amenities of home. The whole idea is to get away from home and rough it for a while. Neither the campers nor I complained because we weren't expecting anything better. Those that complained didn't understand camping. The rest of us realized that the camp was not our home and that we would leave it in a short time. We were at the camp not to settle down, but to accomplish certain tasks and then leave. I was there to speak; they were there to make friends, learn and have fun. After that mission was accomplished, we would all go get comfortable again. With that mindset, putting up with a little discomfort was not difficult at all.

On the other hand, if I had gone to the camp expecting to have all the amenities of home or had gone there with a different objective than I did, I probably would have been miserable and ineffective. However, the fault would have been mine for having improper expectations and for not realizing my true situation.

This is why God was so angry with the Israelites. They should have remembered their situation and their mission and adjusted their mindset accordingly. They were sojourners in the wilderness, traveling campers as it were. That they expected all the comforts of the Promised Land (or Egypt) was not reasonable and showed they had strayed from their mission and forgotten what they were doing. Athletes in the middle of a race and soldiers in the middle of a fight should not expect to feel as comfortable as they do when they are home resting on the sofa. If they start to believe that races and battles should be comfortable, they will certainly lose.

Keeping Your Eyes on the Prize

The second principle goes with the first. Not only do we need to remember that this is not our home, but we also need to focus on the place that is our home. We need to keep remembering the goal of our journey, Heaven. We must keep our eyes on the prize.

Top athletes are driven by one thing: being the best. They are focused on the prize that comes with victory. To win the Tour de France, for example, one must have a single-minded obsession with winning and getting to wear that yellow champion's jersey. Only those who can keep that at the forefront of their thoughts, rather than the pain of the cramping in their thigh, will have a chance.

During their run to the National Hockey League finals in 2003, the coach of the Anaheim Mighty Ducks brought the Stanley Cup into the team's dressing room so that his players could focus on it and envision themselves carrying it around the ice in victory. He wanted them to be clear about what they were sacrificing all their time and effort for. He understood that those who cannot see the goal cannot accomplish it. Of course, keeping your eyes on the prize does not guarantee victory – the Ducks eventually lost – but it certainly makes winning much more likely. Clearly seeing the objective of the struggle is essential.

In the same way, soldiers need to be able to focus on the purpose for which they are fighting. If they can envision the gains a victory will bring, sacrifice will come easier. Soldiers that can focus on the big prize will be able to face the struggle with the strength to make it through the pain.

As soon as soldiers lose sight of that prize (or do not believe there is a reward worth fighting for), all is lost.

Applying this principle to the Exodus story, the Israelites should have kept thinking about Canaan, the land flowing with milk and honey. If they had kept the country of promise at the forefront of their thoughts, they wouldn't have been so bogged down by the troubles that came their way. They needed to be driven, just as any athlete or soldier, by their desire to gain that prize.

For us, this means being driven by the reward of Heaven. We need to have a single-minded obsession with getting to our true home and enjoying that prize. The great men and women of faith certainly did. In fact, the primary characteristic of the heroes listed in Hebrews 11 is their obsession with Heaven. We examined this chapter earlier in the book and noted that faith always results in action. As we survey it again, this time look at what motivated that action. These disciples realized that this world was not their home and they stayed focused on the prize they would receive at the end of their journey.

What Drove the Heroes of Faith

After praising the faith of Abel and Enoch, the author of Hebrews explains that "without faith it is impossible to please God, because anyone who comes to him must believe that he exists and that he rewards those who earnestly seek him" (Hebrews 11:6). Trusting that God will reward his servants is an essential part of faith. Obedience flows from being sure that it will be worth it in the end. We trust that the reward will be great and focus on it as an encouragement to persevere. Look at the Abraham's story, for example:

> By faith Abraham, when called to go to a place he would later receive as his inheritance, obeyed and went, even

though he did not know where he was going. By faith he made his home in the Promised Land like a stranger in a foreign country; he lived in tents, as did Isaac and Jacob, who were heirs with him of the same promise. For he was looking forward to the city with foundations, whose architect and builder is God. (Hebrews 11:8-10)

Abraham lived in tents as a sojourner, just like his descendents later would. And just like they should have but didn't, he accepted his predicament without complaining. There are two reasons he was able to do this: Abraham realized that he wasn't home yet and was focused on the future. He understood that one day he would lay aside his tent for the solid structures of Heaven and he continually looked forward to this reward.

After explaining what motivated Abraham, the author of Hebrews then summarizes the first part of the chapter by explaining that all the rest of the faith heroes were driven by their longing for Heaven as well.

All these people were still living by faith when they died. They did not receive the things promised; they only saw them and welcomed them from a distance. And they admitted that they were aliens and strangers on earth. People who say such things show that they are looking for a country of their own. If they had been thinking of the country they had left, they would have had opportunity to return. Instead, they were longing for a better country – a heavenly one. Therefore God is not ashamed to be called their God, for he has prepared a city for them. (Hebrews 11:13-16)

Here is a perfect example of taking the two measures I have recommended. The people remembered that this world is not their home ("admitted that they were aliens and strangers on earth") and they kept their eyes on Heaven ("they were longing for a better country – a heavenly one"). God was proud to prepare a place for them.

Later in the passage we learn what motivated Moses to give up royalty and identify with his people. He had his eyes on the prize.

> By faith Moses, when he had grown up, refused to be known as the son of Pharaoh's daughter. He chose to be mistreated along with the people of God rather than to enjoy the pleasures of sin for a short time. He regarded disgrace for the sake of Christ as of greater value than the treasures of Egypt, because he was looking ahead to his reward. (Hebrews 11:24-26)

Moses chose to give up the personal peace and prosperity of his life in Pharaoh's palace so that he could gain a much bigger reward. His example was followed by many, many others. In fact, a few verses later we read about men and women who not only met with discomfort, but willingly gave up their lives so that they would gain "a better resurrection." People don't get more Heaven-focused than this:

> Others were tortured and refused to be released, so that they might gain a better resurrection. Some faced jeers and flogging, while still others were chained and put in prison. They were stoned; they were sawed in two; they were put to death by the sword. They went about in sheepskins and goatskins, destitute, persecuted and mistreated – the world was not worthy of them. They wandered in deserts and mountains, and in caves and holes in the ground.

These were all commended for their faith, yet none of them received what had been promised. God had planned something better for us so that only together with us would they be made perfect. (Hebrews 11:35b-40)

"The world was not worthy of them!" What a wonderful way to be remembered. These giants of faith did not receive their reward while on earth, but they weren't expecting it on earth. The reward they had been promised was Heaven.

The practical application for us is clear: "Therefore, since we are surrounded by such a great cloud of witnesses, let us throw off everything that hinders and the sin that so easily entangles, and let us run with perseverance the race marked out for us" (Hebrews 12:1). We are to be like these spiritual masters. We are not to get bogged down by persecutions, the worries of this life and the deceitfulness of wealth. We are not to let the desire for personal peace and prosperity keep us from running the race to the end. We are to keep our eyes firmly on the prize.

To finish the argument, the author of Hebrews then gives us the ultimate example to follow. In the matter of focusing on future rewards to get us through tough times, we are, in fact, to be like Jesus. "Let us fix our eyes on Jesus, the author and perfecter of our faith, who for the joy set before him endured the cross, scorning its shame, and sat down at the right hand of the throne of God. Consider him who endured such opposition from sinful men, so that you will not grow weary and lose heart" (Hebrews 12:2-3).

What enabled Jesus to persevere when he was at his lowest point? The joy set before him! Jesus had a clear vision of the reward he would receive at the end of his service. He saw himself sitting down at the right hand of the throne of God. According to this passage, Jesus was able to withstand the beatings and the cross because he had his mind focused on

Heaven. He had his eyes on the prize. We are to do the same. Setting our eyes on the prize will keep us from growing weary and losing heart in the middle of the wilderness.

Paul so longed to win the prize of Heaven that the thought of sharing in Christ's sufferings to get it was actually appealing to him.

> I want to know Christ and the power of his resurrection and the fellowship of sharing in his sufferings, becoming like him in his death, and so, somehow, to attain to the resurrection from the dead.
>
> Not that I have already obtained all this, or have already been made perfect, but I press on to take hold of that for which Christ Jesus took hold of me. Brothers, I do not consider myself yet to have taken hold of it. But one thing I do: Forgetting what is behind and straining toward what is ahead, I press on toward the goal to win the prize for which God has called me heavenward in Christ Jesus. (Philippians 3:10-14)

Paul didn't spend his life running the race and fighting the fight in order to lose. Paul wanted that reward, and he focused accordingly:

> Do you not know that in a race all the runners run, but only one gets the prize? Run in such a way as to get the prize. Everyone who competes in the games goes into strict training. They do it to get a crown that will not last; but we do it to get a crown that will last forever. Therefore I do not run like a man running aimlessly; I do not fight like a man beating the air. No, I beat my body and make it my slave so that after I have preached

to others, I myself will not be disqualified for the prize. (1 Corinthians 9:24-27)

Paul succeeded in his quest. These are some of his last recorded words:

> For I am already being poured out like a drink offering, and the time has come for my departure. I have fought the good fight, I have finished the race, I have kept the faith. Now there is in store for me the crown of righteousness, which the Lord, the righteous Judge, will award to me on that day – and not only to me, but also to all who have longed for his appearing. (2 Timothy 4:6-8)

Paul longed for the day of Christ's appearing because he knew that would be the day when he would finally get his prize. The race would be over, the battle won. He took this promise of Jesus seriously: "Behold, I am coming soon! My reward is with me, and I will give to everyone according to what he has done" (Revelation 22:12-13).

We need to meditate on that promise at all times. Whenever our vision of that great day becomes blurry, we are in danger of falling into the comfort trap.

Addressing a Possible Objection

Before we leave this chapter, let me quickly address one possible objection. Some people have told me that it seems like I am advocating a mindset that views the reward at the end of our journey as rightful payment for all the suffering we have gone through on the way to getting it. This is not what I am saying at all. The reward of the Promised Land is God's gift. We don't earn it. However, that does not mean that we are not to focus on the fact that we will receive that gift, if we make it through the wilderness, as motivation to persevere. If I tell my daughter she will get to open a special present as soon as she has finished her chores for the day, it does not mean that the present is payment for the chores. However, she can still focus on the present as encouragement and motivation to persevere through her duties. The fact that we have the chance to go to Heaven is an overwhelming act of God's grace. However, that does not make it any less valuable to receive and therefore does not make it any less powerful as a motivating tool.

CHAPTER 13

The Trustworthiness of God

The LORD said to Moses, "How long will these people treat me with contempt? How long will they refuse to believe in me, in spite of all the miraculous signs I have performed among them?"

NUMBERS 14:11

He said to his disciples, "Why are you so afraid? Do you still have no faith?"

MARK 4:35-40

Defeating the desire for personal peace and affluence is not the only thing we need to do to stay on the narrow way. Satan has many more cards to play than that, and we need to counter with a multifaceted battle plan of our own.

One of the devil's most effective attacks involves tempting us to despair by telling us that the path we are on is leading to catastrophe. Naturally, he uses this lie at those times when the future looks bleak: when roadblocks seem insurmountable and the struggle too hard. These are critical moments in life as they force us to decide, "Are we going to live in faith and do what we know God wants us to do, even in the face of much apparent trouble and danger – or not?" Satan comes and whispers in our ear one of his most powerful lies: "God is not trustworthy. Don't do it."

Satan's strategy is to try to bring into doubt God's character or his power. (Satan may also attempt to get you to question other things like God's existence, but this seems to occur less often and be less effective. People don't usually doubt God's existence; they are just not sure about following him.) The deceiver says, "God will let you fall. He will let the water crash in around you. He will let you be defeated by your enemies. He doesn't have your best interests at heart, and even if he does, he doesn't have the ability to make his desires happen. Following him will be disastrous. Don't obey. Don't follow."

Against these lies, it does not help to follow the advice of last chapter and keep our eyes on the prize (although we should keep doing that to combat Satan's other lies), because the reward will not entice us if we are not sure that God is willing and able to come through with it. In combating the devil's attacks on God's trustworthiness, meditating on God's promises is of little use. However, there is something we can do. We can focus on God's faithfulness in the past. As we examine the existing evidence of God's power and goodness, Satan's attempt at sabotaging our journey will be seen for the ruse that it is.

If only more of the Israelites had followed this principle. Their experience at the very edge of the Promised Land provides another stellar example of what not to do.

Doubt at Kadesh Barnea

The journey of the Israelites finally seemed to be near an end. They had reached the border of Canaan and camped at a place called Kadesh Barnea. At God's request, Moses chose 12 men to spy out the land in preparation for conquest.

When Moses sent them to explore Canaan, he said, "Go up through the Negev and on into the hill country. See what the land is like and whether the people who live there are strong or weak, few or many. What kind of land do they live in? Is it good or bad? What kind of towns do they live in? Are they unwalled or fortified? How is the soil? Is it fertile or poor? Are there trees on it or not? Do your best to bring back some of the fruit of the land." (It was the season for the first ripe grapes.)

So they went up and explored the land from the Desert of Zin as far as Rehob, toward Lebo Hamath. They went up through the Negev and came to Hebron, where Ahiman, Sheshai and Talmai, the descendants of Anak, lived. (Hebron had been built seven years before Zoan in Egypt.) When they reached the Valley of Eshcol, they cut off a branch bearing a single cluster of grapes. Two of them carried it on a pole between them, along with some pomegranates and figs. That place was called the Valley of Eshcol because of the cluster of grapes the Israelites cut off there. At the end of forty days they returned from exploring the land.

They came back to Moses and Aaron and the whole Israelite community at Kadesh in the Desert of Paran. There they reported to them and to the whole assembly and showed them the fruit of the land. They gave Moses this account: "We went into the land to which you sent us, and it does flow with milk and honey! Here is its fruit. But the people who live there are powerful, and the cities are fortified and very large. We even saw descendants of Anak there. The Amalekites live in the Negev; the Hittites, Jebusites and Amorites live in the hill country; and the Canaanites live near the sea and along the Jordan."

Then Caleb silenced the people before Moses and said, "We should go up and take possession of the land, for we can certainly do it."

But the men who had gone up with him said, "We can't attack those people; they are stronger than we are." And they spread among the Israelites a bad report about the land they had explored. They said, "The land we explored devours those living in it. All the people we saw there are of great size. We saw the Nephilim there (the descendants of Anak come from the Nephilim). We seemed like grasshoppers in our own eyes, and we looked the same to them."

That night all the people of the community raised their voices and wept aloud. All the Israelites grumbled against Moses and Aaron, and the whole assembly said to them, "If only we had died in Egypt! Or in this desert! Why is the LORD bringing us to this land only to let us fall by the sword? Our wives and children will be taken as plunder. Wouldn't it be better for us to go back to Egypt?" And they said to each other, "We should choose a leader and go back to Egypt."

Then Moses and Aaron fell facedown in front of the whole Israelite assembly gathered there. Joshua son of Nun and Caleb son of Jephunneh, who were among those who had explored the land, tore their clothes and said to the entire Israelite assembly, "The land we passed through and explored is exceedingly good. If the Lord is pleased with us, he will lead us into that land, a land flowing with milk and honey, and will give it to us. Only do not rebel against the Lord. And do not be afraid of the people of the land, because we will swallow them up. Their protection is gone, but the Lord is with us. Do not be afraid of them."

But the whole assembly talked about stoning them. (Numbers 13:17-14:10a)

The Israelites were at a critical point of decision. God had told them to take the land, but they were afraid of its current inhabitants. The obstacles to victory looked too big. In other words, they simply didn't think God had the ability or willingness to do what he had promised and conquer their enemies and therefore they didn't want to obey. They didn't think God could be trusted. Of the spies, only Caleb and Joshua believed God could do it. These men, along with Moses and Aaron, were eager to take the land, but they could not convince the rest of the people.

As a result, God sent the Hebrews back out into the wilderness to wander for forty years. None of the people (20 years old or older) who grumbled against God got to enter the land. They all died in the desert (Numbers 14:26-35).

The Israelites believed Satan's lie. They succumbed to irrational fear. I say their fear was irrational because the people were not being asked to take a blind leap of faith at Kadesh Barnea. God wasn't new to them. They hadn't just met him. The people should have known that God was trustworthy. They had seen his power and goodness over and over again. He had always been faithful to take care of them in any and every situation. All they needed to do was remember this, and they would have been fine. They had plenty of good reasons to trust in him.

This is what made God so angry. He had given them abundant evidence of his trustworthiness, yet they still wouldn't step out in faith and obey.

> Then the glory of the LORD appeared at the Tent of Meeting to all the Israelites. The LORD said to Moses, "How long will these people treat me with contempt? How long will they refuse to believe in me, in spite of all the miraculous signs I have performed among them? I will strike them down with a plague and destroy them, but I will make you into a nation greater and stronger than they." (Numbers 14:10b-12)

In spite of all the miraculous signs, in spite of all the evidence of God's power and goodness, the Israelites refused to trust.

The Power of Praise

There is a simple antidote to fear of the future and lack of faith in God: praising him for what he has done in the past. Instead of grumbling and cowering at the report of giant cities and powerful men, the Israelites should have had a time of prayer and praise, thanking God for his wonderful work in getting them to this point. After spending some time remembering the plagues and the Red Sea and the provision of manna from Heaven and water from the rock and the victory over the Amalekites, etc., they almost certainly would have been willing to enter the land expecting to see God perform more miracles.

The act of recounting the stories and thanking God for what he has done puts a person in the frame of mind necessary to obediently step out in faith. It shines the light of truth on the present situation and destroys the lie that God is not trustworthy.

You may recall that this is exactly what happened in the story of King Jehoshaphat that we covered in Chapter 6. Judah looked as if it was going to be overrun by a powerful army. Rather than despair, however, the king called the people together for prayer and praise.

Then Jehoshaphat stood up in the assembly of Judah and Jerusalem at the temple of the LORD in the front of the new courtyard and said:

"O LORD, God of our fathers, are you not the God who is in heaven? You rule over all the kingdoms of the nations. Power and might are in your hand, and no one can withstand you. O our God, did you not drive out the inhabitants of this land before your people Israel and give it forever to the descendants of Abraham your friend? They have lived in it and have built in it a sanctuary for your Name, saying, 'If calamity comes upon us, whether the sword of judgment, or plague or famine, we will stand in your presence before this temple that bears your Name and will cry out to you in our distress, and you will hear us and save us.'

"But now here are men from Ammon, Moab and Mount Seir, whose territory you would not allow Israel to invade when they came from Egypt; so they turned away from them and did not destroy them. See how they are repaying us by coming to drive us out of the possession you gave us as an inheritance. O our God, will you not judge them? For we have no power to face this vast army that is attacking us. We

do not know what to do, but our eyes are upon you."
(2 Chronicles 20:5-12)

Notice the confidence inspiring content of the prayer. Jehoshaphat started by ascribing to God all power and then backed up this claim by recounting what God had done in the past in giving Israel the land. With his mind focused on God's faithfulness in the past, Jehoshaphat could look confidently towards the future, knowing that God is trustworthy and will keep his promises. When asked to step out in faith and face the army, Jehoshaphat obeyed, even though it looked like a fool's errand, and God provided a great victory (2 Chronicles 20:14-29).

God would have done the same for the Israelites at Kadesh Barnea, but they refused to remember all that he had done and were therefore unwilling to obey in faith. They focused on the strength of the enemy rather than the strength of God. In later years their ancestors would make the same mistake in the valley of Elah. Thankfully, there was one among them who had experienced and remembered God's power and goodness.

David and Goliath

It is one of the most famous tales in the history of the world, but let's take a moment to reacquaint ourselves with the story of David and Goliath.

Israel was at war with the Philistines and the two armies had drawn up battle lines on either side of the Valley of Elah, with the Philistines employing an interesting strategy.

A champion named Goliath, who was from Gath, came out of the Philistine camp. He was over nine feet tall. He had a bronze helmet on his head and wore a coat of scale armor of bronze weighing five thousand shekels; on his legs he wore bronze greaves, and a bronze javelin was slung on his back. His spear shaft was like a weaver's rod, and its iron point weighed six hundred shekels. His shield bearer went ahead of him.

Goliath stood and shouted to the ranks of Israel, "Why do you come out and line up for battle? Am I not a Philistine, and are you not the servants of Saul? Choose a man and have him come down to me. If he is able to fight and kill me, we will become your subjects; but if I overcome him and kill him, you will become our subjects and serve us." Then the Philistine said, "This day I defy the ranks of Israel! Give me a man and let us fight each other." On hearing the Philistine's words, Saul and all the Israelites were dismayed and terrified. (1 Samuel 17:4-11)

This taunting continued for over a month until one day the shepherd boy David arrived to check on his brothers and see how the battle was going (1 Samuel 17:16-20). While David was talking with the troops, Goliath made his daily appearance within earshot of the youngster (1 Samuel 17:23). David asked around about what would be done for the man who killed Goliath and word of his inquiries got back to King Saul, who summoned David (1 Samuel 17:25-31).

In the discussion that followed, notice what gave David the confidence to face Goliath. David was not afraid of the mighty soldier because he was aware of what God had done for David in the past.

David said to Saul, "Let no one lose heart on account of this Philistine; your servant will go and fight him."

Saul replied, "You are not able to go out against this Philistine and fight him; you are only a boy, and he has been a fighting man from his youth."

But David said to Saul, "Your servant has been keeping his father's sheep. When a lion or a bear came and carried off a sheep from the flock, I went after it, struck it and rescued the sheep from its mouth. When it turned on me, I seized it by its hair, struck it and killed it. Your servant has killed both the lion and the bear; this uncircumcised Philistine will be like one of them, because he has defied the armies of the living God. The LORD who delivered me from the paw of the lion and the paw of the bear will deliver me from the hand of this Philistine."

Saul said to David, "Go, and the LORD be with you." (1 Samuel 17:32-37)

David knew that God was able to help him defeat Goliath because God had helped him defeat strong enemies before. While everyone else looked at Goliath and saw only certain defeat, David remembered what God had done to the bear and the lion and saw sure victory. By keeping his mind on God's past mighty works, David was able to affirm God's trustworthiness and take a huge step of faith with confidence.

David was in the very same position as the Israelites at Kadesh Barnea. Both were faced with the option of either following God and stepping into battle with a very strong foe or turning around and running in fear. David looked back, realized God was trustworthy, and took a step of faith. The Israelites didn't. They looked only at the obstacle in front of them, never looking back at what God had done, and ended up dying in the desert for lack of faith.

May we follow the example of David and not the Israelites. The longer we walk with Jesus and experience his power and goodness, the stronger our faith should be. When faced with one of those situations that seems sure to end in catastrophe, we should be able to look back at all God has done and face the future with confidence, knowing he can handle it.

Jesus Calms the Storm

Jesus' disciples were a little slow in learning this lesson, as demonstrated in the following episode.

> That day when evening came, he said to his disciples, "Let us go over to the other side." Leaving the crowd behind, they took him along, just as he was, in the boat. There were also other boats with him. A furious squall came up, and the waves broke over the boat, so that it was nearly swamped. Jesus was in the stern, sleeping on a cushion. The disciples woke him and said to him, "Teacher, don't you care if we drown?"
>
> He got up, rebuked the wind and said to the waves, "Quiet! Be still!" Then the wind died down and it was completely calm.
>
> He said to his disciples, "Why are you so afraid? Do you still have no faith?" (Mark 4:35-40)

The important word in that last sentence is "still." The key to understanding Jesus' rebuke is to realize that the disciples had already seen Jesus do many miraculous signs and wonders. He had shown his power and goodness in casting out demons and healing many sick and lame (Mark 1:21-3:12). The proper response to the storm would have been to remember that Jesus had been willing and able to exert authority over every other realm of existence (see Chapter 2), and surmise that he could handle this, too. The disciples obviously did not do this, as they were convinced that death was immanent.

Remembering God's faithfulness is a very difficult thing to do, especially when the wind is blowing hard and it seems like the waves will swamp us, but we must do it if we are ever going to stride boldly into the Promised Land.

Finally Home

Striding boldly into the Promised Land is exactly what Joshua did 40 years after the debacle at Kadesh Barnea. One of the two spies who trusted God, Joshua had the privilege of finally leading the Israelites into Canaan. As we conclude this chapter and this book, let me encourage you with the words that God gave to Joshua as he prepared to cross the Jordon River into Canaan.

> Your territory will extend from the desert to Lebanon, and from the great river, the Euphrates – all the Hittite country – to the Great Sea on the west. No one will be able to stand up against you all the days of your life. As I was with Moses, so I will be with you; I will never leave you nor forsake you.

> Be strong and courageous, because you will lead these people to inherit the land I swore to their fore-fathers to give them. Be strong and very courageous. Be careful to obey all the law my servant Moses gave you; do not turn from it to the right or to the left, that you may be successful wherever you go. Do not let this Book of the Law depart from your mouth; medi-tate on it day and night, so that you may be careful to do everything written in it. Then you will be pros-

perous and successful. Have I not commanded you? Be strong and courageous. Do not be terrified; do not be discouraged, for the LORD your God will be with you wherever you go. (Joshua 1:4-9)

The narrow road to Heaven is long and difficult and full of traps, but you can travel it successfully because God will be with you. Be strong and courageous. Fight the good fight. Finish the race. I'll see you at home.

Notes

1. www.tcsdaily.com/article.aspx?id=041905A.

2. Gregg Easterbrook, *The Progress Paradox: How Life Gets Better While People Feel Worse* (New York: Random House, 2004), xiii-xiv.

3. Easterbrook, xiv-xv.

4. Easterbrook, xv-xvi.

5. I will not take time here to present the full "argument from desire." I encourage everyone to read *Mere Christianity* by C.S. Lewis for proper treatment of this subject.

6. C.S. Lewis, *Mere Christianity* (New York: Collier Books, 1960), 120.

7. When I use the term "Heaven" in this book, I am using it in a general sense to refer to that state of existence in which those that are saved will live for eternity. I am not making dogmatic assertions about the specific

nature of that existence other than to say it will be perfect because we will be with God. For the purposes of this book, I am defining Heaven as simply the "life" spoken of in Matthew 7:14.

8. Randy Alcorn, *Heaven* (Wheaton: Tyndale, 2004), 160.

9. G.K Chesterton, *Orthodoxy* (Chicago: Thomas More Association, 1985), 99-100.

10. This is taken from the Monday, July 10, 2006, posting at "Daily Reflections," the Bible study aid published on the *Touchstone* magazine web site (http://www.touchstonemag.com/frpat.html).

11. For a nicely balanced short article on the three tenses of salvation, see "Salvation: Past, Present of Future?" in Walter C. Kaiser Jr., Peter H. Davids, F.F. Bruce, and Manfred T. Brauch, *The Hard Sayings of The Bible* (Downers Grove: InterVarsity Press, 1996), 709-710. According to the Bible, Christians have been saved, are being saved and will be saved, with the emphasis on the future tense.

12. Dietrich Bonhoeffer, *The Cost of Discipleship* (New York: Touchstone, 1995), 89.

13. I owe the phrases "God's delight in being God" and "God's passion for his glory," as well as much of this argument, to John Piper, *God's Passion for His Glory* (Wheaton: Crossway, 1998).

14. Jonathan Edwards, *The Religious Affections*, John Smith, ed., *The Works of Jonathan Edwards*, vol. 2 (New Haven: Yale University Press, 1959), 249-50.

15. Piper, 34-35.

16. Piper, 32.

17. Bonhoeffer, 63.

18. www.youthpastor.com/lessons/index.cfm/WWJD_if_ he_experienced_problems_or_pain_227.htm.

19. This insight into the nature of the testing at Massah and its relationship to Jesus' temptation comes from my friend and partner Brandon Ridley.

20. Lewis, 80.

21. For those unfamiliar with this term, it refers to an upgrade package that one can purchase when buying a new car. It usually includes leather seats and other extra features not found on base models.

22. For a fuller discussion of the poll data, see Ronald J. Sider, *The Scandal of the Evangelical Conscience* (Grand Rapids, Baker, 2005).

23. www.blazinggrace.org/pornstatistics.htm.

24. Sider, 17.

25. I am not here making any dogmatic statements about the nature of baptism. Regardless of whether "baptism" refers to different modes of water baptism or baptism by the Holy Spirit, the point I am making here is that there is a clear parallel between the Christian walk and the Hebrew journey and that neither is complete at the point of baptism.

26. Arthur W. Pink, *Studies on Saving Faith* (Swengel, PA, Reiner Publications, publication date unknown. The Publisher's "Preface" states: "To give the reader a clearer appreciation of this book, it should be stated that the materials found herein were first published in 1932, 1933, and 1937, in *Studies in the Scriptures*, a monthly magazine published by Mr. Pink from 1922 to 1953.") The full text of this book is readily available for free on the internet. This particular quotation can be found at www.pbministries.org/books/pink/ Saving_Faith/saving_faith_part1.htm.

27. Charles H Spurgeon, *Morning and Evening*, February 8 Evening. This book is also public domain and readily available for free on the internet. One place to find it is www.ccel.org/ccel/spurgeon/morneve.html.

28. Christine A. Scheller, "A Divine Conspirator," *Christianity Today* vol. 50, no. 9 (2006), 45.

29. Francis A. Schaffer, *How Should We Then Live* (Wheaton: Crossway, 1976), 205.

Printed in the United States
77425LV00003B/109-999